in memory of
HOYT W. FULLER
1923-1981

Woodie King, Jr., founder and producer, and Mayme Mitcham, production coordinator, of the New Federal Theatre, Henry Street Settlement, New York City, 1973.

Black Theatre

by Woodie King, Jr.

Present Condition

National Black Theatre Touring Circuit

The author is grateful for permission to reprint the articles included here. Their sources, with original title and year of publication are:

Negro Digest: "On Being a Black Actor in White America," originally "Problems Facing Negro Actors," 1966; "Black Theatre for Black Communities," originally "The Arts, Youth, and Social Changes," 1967; "Langston's Leaving Never Meant He Was Gone," originally "Remembering Langston Hughes," 1969; "We Must Break with European Traditions," originally "Will Black Theatre Please Stand and Take a Bow?" 1970.

The Drama Review: "Bringing an End to the Theft of Black Art" originally "Black Theatre Present Condition," 1968.

Black World: "The Failure of Educational Theatre," originally "Educational Theatre and the Black Community," 1972; "New York Is Not the Answer," originally "Stage, Screen, and Black Hegemony," 1975; "How *Winesellers* Came to the Stage: Log of a Hit," originally "Directing Winesellers," 1976.

Black Theatre Alliance *Newsletter:* "Alive and Well and In Your Neighborhood," originally "The Black Theatre Movement, 3 Tonys, Why?" 1974; "We Must Sustain Our Own Theatres," originally Black Theatre Alliance *Newsletter* interview, 1977.

Black Scholar: "Sacred Songs: Rhythm and Blues and Yesterday," originally "Searching for Brothers Kindred: Rhythm and Blues in the 1950s," 1974.

Easy: "How the Movement Got Started," originally *Easy* interview, 1978.

First World: "Anatomy of a Successful Play," originally "Producing Commercial Theatre," 1978.

Freedomways: "Legacy of *A Raisin:* Hansberry's Children" originally "Lorraine Hansberry's Children: Black Artist and *A Raisin in the Sun,"* 1979.

Players: "A Conversation with Woodie King, Jr." originally *Players* interview, 1980.

Library of Congress Cataloging in Publication Data

King, Woodie.
    Black theatre present condition.

    1. Afro-American theatre.   I. Title.
PN2270.A35K5   792'.08996073   81-14141
ISBN 0-89062-133-0   AACR2

All photographs by Bert Andrews.
Produced by Publishing Center for Cultural Resources, New York City.
Manufactured in the United States of America.

Contents

On Being a Black Actor
in White America

THE PROBLEMS OF THE NEGRO ACTOR
are not so much the Negro actor's problem as they are the white American
problem. When an American Negro actor is faced with playing a character, he
must also confront a trio of problems. First, should the character be American
in its truest sense? (When American life is most American it is apt to be most
theatrical, says Ralph Ellison.) Second, should he be Negro as Negroes really
are or Negro as we have led whites to believe we are in order to endure? And
third, should the character be American Negro? (The peculiar sensation—
double-consciousness—an American, a Negro: W. E. B. Du Bois.) These
problems are not easily solved since white America has already told us what
the answers are going to be if we intend to act on *its* stage.

An old Negro actor told me he hated LeRoi Jones' two plays *The Slave*
and *The Toilet* because they were too filled with protest. His student, a young
beginner, agreed with him even to the point of accusing the plays of being
vulgar. The strange thing was that the beginner had no idea of the kind of plays
or the problems the old actor faced during the thirties and forties, no idea of the
vast history of his craft. (I will get back to this a little later.) It was a strange
conversation. The old actor putting down Jones for protest writing and at the
same time telling me: "Acting in the thirties had life, vitality... Federal
Theatre... Negro *Macbeth*... *Roll, Sweet Chariot*... *Run Little Children*.
And the actors! Leigh Whipper, Edna Thomas... son, you oughta been
there!"

Beginners. Interested beginners view bad road companies, inexperienced
stock companies, and cute community food digesters. These prospective
actors watch plays and actors that say absolutely nothing. The parts the actors
play are not worth the time and efforts put into them. Beginners watch plays
that do not attempt to recreate our experiences; they watch cute white plays
because that is all white America wants.

Dudder Love cast, New York City, 1972.

A Negro actor can sometimes be found in these cute little comedies— *Anniversary Waltz, Come Blow Your Horn, Enter Laughing, Kiss and Tell,* or something similar. His first lines set the Negro beginner's teeth on edge. The embarrassed prospective actor glances about the white theater. All the white faces are laughing at the excessive and ridiculous mannerisms the white director has given the Negro actor. If he makes it, the beginner is thinking, this must not happen to him. He must do exactly as the white actors else the audience will laugh at him simply for being a Negro on the stage, too. But the beginner doesn't know that white people, in general, don't know enough about Negro life to know which details to look for, how to absorb the interpretation the Negro actor wants to present.

After reading more plays and "how to act" books, he assumes that he is ready to be Henry Fonda, Marlon Brando, Sidney Poitier, Cary Grant, Sir Laurence Olivier, etc. He scouts until he finds a white theatre group needing a flat painter, carpenter, coffee boy, etc. However, before he can get this job, he must be able to intellectually discuss Sartre, Albee, Pinter, Beckett, Brecht, and Stanislavski.

He can name a hundred white actors, but he can't name five Negro actors. This is a sad fact. Recently, I talked to a young actress who is paying a great deal of money for acting and singing lessons. She had never heard of W.C. Handy or Charlie Parker! And knew absolutely nothing about the history of the Negro theatre. Yet the beginner can tell one everything—after two months with the white group—about the white theatre. He will argue about staging a play, about what a writer means, about the way he would tackle a role if he ever played one.

Finally, the little social group will do a little comedy and the Negro beginner will be given a cute little "buddy" part. And the white audiences will laugh at him exactly as they had done at the plays he had watched that featured professional Negro actors.

The beginner will eventually learn the truth about all the little social groups. He will begin to doubt when white beginners continue to get leading roles, no matter how bad they are, while he paints sets and occasionally is rewarded with a walk-on or a "buddy" part. Or perhaps it will be while reading J. Marriott's massive book on the theatre in which the author warns beginners (whites) against getting *with those little groups and working like a nigger* forever. He learns after about two years of hard labor that Sartre and Beckett are only talk with these little groups. And that they had no intention of using him except as comic relief.

University Theatre. The Negro actor enrolls, believing he will appear in the plays because he will be a student paying tuition to learn all phases of the theatre. However, he will not be taught all phases of theatre at a university, least of all acting. Again he is left out because the selections are mostly classics or some other form of archaic theatre that was written when the Black man did not figure into the scheme of white America. And we know that the professors who select the plays are white, therefore personal idiosyncrasies enter into the problem. And they keep the Negro actor from the stage. The basic motive is simply resentment towards miscegenation on the American stage in general and the university stage in particular. America doesn't want the Negro actor to be a man on its stage.

And since the basic themes of American plays revolve around sex, the Negro actor's situation is tragic. The student obtains nothing at all. How can he when the acted-out play on stage before an audience is the basic dynamics of such a course of study? The true understanding of acting comes when the student is involved in acting and producing before a live audience. And the professors destroy this by selecting classics which the Negro actor finds difficulty in acting, not to mention the difficulty of casting. "I can't use you in this one Mr. Black It's a Swedish (or Russian, Norwegian, French, etc.) play."

The majority of Negro actors who seek training in university theatre have traces of the southern dialect if they have not acquired a standard white accent. And the way American education is today, one cannot have any traces of the South in speech. It is an awful but true fact. What, then, if the student actor is cast because of necessity in *Three Sisters, Enemy of the People, Antigone, St. Joan, Major Barbara....* ? Can he be convincing in such a dated repertory which was written when he did not figure into the scheme of things?

A drama department must seek "truths" in theatrical works. Many professors keep these "truths" in mind when casting, and very often avoid the Negro actor. The Negro actor cannot bring "truth" (as whites see it) to the classics.

However, a university will—if the National Association for the Advancement of Colored People complains—present *Emperor Jones* or *Othello.* And *maybe* the *Merchant of Venice* after consulting the local synagogue. But a Negro actor cannot look forward to playing a lead character in a university theatre production. After graduating, he knows nothing about acting before an audience.

Item: I compared the average ratio of plays a Negro actor appeared in per season to the average number a white actor appeared in per season at Wayne State University in Detroit. I also compared the total number of plays of Negro graduates against white graduates. The ratio was 1 to 17.

Drama School. The only place to obtain acting experience is the drama school. The Negro actor either goes to a theatre magazine or obtains information from a friend in the theatre: both stress how great the instructor is at teaching Mr. Stanislavski's method. The actor finds his past acting experience brushed aside by the teacher. He is immediately tossed into a beginner's class. If he is above average (better than every white actor in the class) he will work with some "name professionals." If not, he will work with a teacher who has no knowledge at all about the Negro, and very little about acting.

The teacher knows that established names are impressive to the new actor. He will occasionally mention the times he worked with Jesse Bonstelle, Poitier, Garrick, Fiske, Modjeska, Brando, or Beaumont and Fletcher (not necessarily in this order). Yet, the drama schools, with all their faults, are the only places where a Negro actor can sharpen his craft. This, of course, is because he actually works on a stage with others before a live audience.

Now, after a long and arduous journey, the young Negro aspirant becomes a professional actor. Some use the achievements of the past to guide their future. I said earlier I would get back to this. Now it is all right to be of the present; no one would knock this; but when a performer knows absolutely nothing of the history of his profession, how can he possibly understand the present? The most proficient actors in the business — Sidney Poitier, Robert Hooks, Al Freeman, Jr., Diana Sands, Cliff Frazier, Brock Peters, Ivan Dixon, Abby Lincoln, Gloria Foster, Clarence Williams III, Roscoe Lee Browne — know the past and present, and have ideas of some of the future problems they will encounter.

The photos by Carl Van Vechten and Vandamm of the late Charles Gilpin, Rose McClendon, Canada Lee, Frank Wilson, Jack Carter, Edna Thomas, Abbie Mitchell, and Freda Washington are the perfect examples of the glory of the past. They were the actors who brought forth to America the famous all-Negro productions of *Macbeth, Porgy, Haiti,* and other exciting plays via the Federal Theater Project. It grew out of Harlem, and it remains to this day an important contribution to the American stage. I think it is because those actors had a purpose. So many of today's actors lack purpose and direction. How can one grasp for something when there is nothing to grasp? Shout in rage if not really angry? And too, one cannot communicate and assimilate at the same time.

Item: In the midst of the present racial struggle in this country, our stage ignores it. It treats it as if it doesn't exist.

Negro Playwright. The Negro actor's situation can be bettered by (1) joining with Negro writers and (2) building an audience within the Negro community. I think this has been done with great results in Detroit at the Concept-East Theater and in Harlem with LeRoi Jones' Black Arts Theater. Both actor and playwright must be willing to experiment with new forms within their respective crafts. If this is done, the small churches and corner storefronts will be filled with willing ears. And it can be done since there is no one to answer to but each other. It worked in Harlem with the American Negro Theater; they produced Phillip Yordan's *Anna Lucasta* with great results. It produced worthy plays by Negro writers: Abram Hill's *On Strivers Row,* and early plays by young Ossie Davis. And twenty years later Mr. Davis hit Broadway with his romping comedy, *Purlie Victorious.* Now Ossie Davis is an experienced writer; not one of the typical "library writers" (Clifford Odets) but one who has the background in acting and directing within a Negro community.

And if we do not know yet that a play about Negroes must appeal to Negroes, we should leave the theatre. I do not mean they must love or hate it. But they must *identify* with it.

The playwright must seize new ideas and techniques if the Negro actor is to again be of any importance. He must disregard the argument he received in college—an argument for a standardization which is paradoxically strangling the actor's contribution.

Item: The plays of the early Abbey Theatre in Dublin were not considered excellent unless they caused a riot. The theatre, as it is today, without controversy and excitement (save LeRoi Jones), is dead theatre. It is a place to go and digest dinner.

The Negro playwright should write about what he understands. All around him, he can see what happens when white writers pen Negro "struggle situations." They all fail due to a lack of understanding the subject.

As a Negro playwright tells it, explaining to James Baldwin how Ketti Fring came to adapt Richard Wright's *Long Dream:* "She was sitting by this swimming pool, dig, and reading this book and she thought, 'This would make a perfectly darling play!' So she wrote the first few scenes and called out her butler, chauffeur, and maid and read the first few scenes to them and asked, 'Now, isn't this the way you poor, downtrodden, colored people feel about things?'

" 'Why, yes Miss Fring!' they answered, *after considering which is better, keeping Miss Fring happy or disliking the play* (italics mine). 'And, I thought so,' says the playwright. 'And on we go. And on and on.' "

All the critics felt approximately the same about it after it opened on Broadway. Here, in part, is one example from John Chapman: "...I did depart after the first act of this one and reported to my newspaper that this act of *The Long Dream* was shoddy and lascivious— a degradation of my seat companion and of several admirable Negro actors...It seemed impossible that this play could have been adapted by the lady who did such a beautiful job of adapting Thomas Wolfe's *Look Homeward Angel*."

Of course the better things about the play were omitted by Mr. Chapman. The brilliant direction by Lloyd Richards; and the two excellent performances by Al Freeman and Lawrence Winters.

A similar thing happened when Baldwin wrote *Blues For Mr. Charlie*. All his white characters were badly drawn; and many thought this would have been impossible for Baldwin to do, since it is he who stresses always that *Negroes know more about whites than whites know of themselves. Negroes have been taking care of their children and kitchens for over three hundred years.*

I also think that more Negro novelists should write for the theatre. If *The Long Dream, The Cool World, Mandingo,* etc., are dramatized then it should be John O. Killens, Ronald Fair, William Melvin Kelley, Chester Himes or some Negro writer doing the adapting. And even though Baldwin failed with his white characters, his Negro characters were so real and vivid that one is held spellbound by them.

Let me say this in conclusion: If the Negro actor can impose his own values upon the American stage, namely, his past, present, and possible future, he can join with white America in controlling it.

Black Theatre
for Black Communities

"...*The age we live in is very complex...things exist because man lets them.*"
August Heckscher, Director
Twentieth Century Fund

THEATRE FOR SOCIAL WELFARE has replaced theatre's old image—an image of pastime activity. The federal government is subsidizing many of the country's repertory theatres, however no Black theatres. And the present funded repertory theatres are not involving talents from the Black communities. There should be an involvement of the Black communities in this new awareness of the power of the theatres, because the social condition of this country is directly related to conditions in the Black communities. To say that *Barefoot in the Park* and *Hello Dolly!* represent theatre is, in a sense, like saying Black communities do not exist. It is a paradox to expect that "nonexistent" community to come "downtown" to Broadway or to the Tyrone Guthrie Theatre (in Minneapolis) and pay to support what has no relation at all to what the members of that community know as this society.

Item: Witness *The Odd Couple, Any Wednesday, I Do! I Do!, Mame!*

Art for profit, or a play by Jean Kerr, has never been a password from Black talents. They are not that far removed from the lifeline. But it is not the Black talents that are funded or even encouraged to be a part of the federally supported repertory theatres. The repertory companies are encouraged by the boards of education and the poverty programs to perform in the school systems and before the culturally deprived; yet, the plays and the artists are far removed from the lifeline of the Black communities.

In New York and California, there are cultural programs operating under the Anti-Poverty Program. These drama and dance companies could easily operate in conjunction with the boards of education to bring socially meaningful art to local schools. It seems to me that a theatre for the social welfare of communities should provide opportunities for talented Blacks *in* the communities to develop as artists within a professional setting. At the same time, this could demonstrate the need for community-based repertory. Both talent and theatre would be making a collective contribution to the community. This is not happening.

The artists who are supported create from a safe distance; therefore, their work is synthetic. Their description of this society, their attempt to make order out of chaos, has no lasting value. How can an artists depict a Black art, say of Watts, Mississippi, or Harlem, when that artist is living comfortably in Westport or Hollywood?

Item: The federal government under Title 1 and Title 3 is supporting Stuart Vaughn's New Orleans Repertory Theatre. No Negroes are involved—neither in background or foreground.

It has been proven that a Black audience does exist for a socially meaningful theatre. Blacks came out to support Baldwin's *Blues for Mister Charlie* and *Amen Corner;* they supported Hansberry's *A Raisin in the Sun,* LeRoi Jones' Black Arts Repertory and his one-act plays, *The Toilet, The Slave,* and *Dutchman;* now they are flocking to Douglas Turner Ward's *Happy Ending* and *Day of Absence.* These plays could easily belong to a Black, federally-supported repertory theatre in a Black community. For integration, a Black Hamlet, Genet's *The Blacks,* or Duberman's *In White America.* Otherwise, Black talent will continue to wait for white approval on projects that are watered, rewritten, or rejected, labeled "protest."

Oppressed people and classes have historically channeled their images and passions to the stage. Beaumarchais' *Marriage of Figaro* kindled social fires that helped flame the French Revolution. Gorky's *The Lower Depths,* in 1902, dramatized the oppression of Russia's peasants. Clifford Odets, during the thirties, stung the social conscience with his pro-labor play, *Waiting For Lefty.*

Item: Art must deal with the time. My students here at Mobilization For Youth were so moved by *Waiting For Lefty* that they adapted it from the original cab strike to a rent strike on New York's Lower East Side. Something meaningful for them.

There must be some reason for not showing the young and the deprived what the theatre is capable of doing. Could it be fear?

There must be a change in the identity of those who bring art into the Black communities if Blacks are to have quality education and participation in the various art forms, including theatre. Even now, the Lincoln Center Repertory Company is taking live theatre into the New York school system and to the "culturally deprived." While it is effective in the schools that are basically middle class, it is less effective in the schools, say in Harlem and Bedford Stuyvesant. This is because whites believe that Blacks are still trying to assimilate; it is the exact reverse. On the ascendant now is a tremendous pride in being Black. Whites' ignorance of this is causing ineffectual education, and, of course, the promotion of subject matter that is boring to the children in these areas. In the theatre of the sixties, Black consciousness has reached new levels of concentration and intensity. A metaphysical play by Beckett with Negro and Puerto Rican performers would be more effective than Shakespeare with an all-white cast because Blacks would immediately identify with the visual image of the present.

Item: In Harlem, Roger Furman, operating with Office of Economic Opportunity funds as a part of HARYOU, has consistently exhibited fine theatre; his productions with young, vital performers would be an inspiration for every junior high school student in the ghetto.

After reading the reports from the Ford Foundation in the 1960's and the Rockefeller Foundation, one can hardly find reasons why they should not have dumped grants into these socially deprived communities. The foundations state their policies, which do not hold generally for Black communities. Example:

The Foundation should exercise discrimination and selectivity and give its funds largely for significant activity not likely to be supported by others.

They should seek out, sustain, and amplify excellence and, where necessary, create new centers of excellence.

They should help to increase the vigor of private institutions and private initiative in areas of critical concern to society.

There are some twenty-five regional theatres in the United States supported by foundations and the federal government under the National Endowment of the Arts, and Titles 1 and 3 under the Elementary and Secondary Education Act. These theatres do not include Blacks on staff as designers, directors, writers, or technicians. Black actors are booked in as spear carriers in the old classics. Nothing is realistic in these regional theatres for the Black artist; nothing is realistic for Black audiences. Now the federal government is helping to support this discriminating system.

It started in the middle fifties after the McCarthy Senate investigations. Pop Art emerged because the artist could say it meant *A* when it really meant *B*, or vice versa. Art, as well as the theatre, went abstract for safety— "happenings," "theatre of the absurd," etc. It became a lie; artists knew this; the public knew it. It could not last. Black artists emerged from the chaos because they had less to lose; white America went deeper into it by trying to escape via musicals, comedies, British "angry young men," *and because* the country was afraid, it laughed and danced, trying to forget the lie.

The social welfare of this country is at stake. White America, trying to escape from the inner city to the suburb, is synonymous to whites trying to escape from what we all know can exist: *order in the chaos*. Under all that singing and dancing on Broadway, there is a lifeline: Vietnam, Mississippi, Harlem, Watts, Malcolm X.

Theatre is no longer a pastime. It is serious business. It can be dangerous. And yet, we know that Black communities must have their own art centers, because white values are not Black values.

In the thirties, when Roosevelt's Works Progress Administration (WPA) supported the theatre, Blacks were *involved* because the theatre put money in circulation. Blacks didn't control it as many believe. It was, on the whole, meaningful, even though in the eyes of Roosevelt's Administration it was pastime activity, "high class."

Theatre for social welfare was disguised as pastime activity until the Establishment witnessed performances of *The Cradle Will Rock, It Can't Happen Here, One Third of the Nation*. But now, during the sixties, theatre for pastime activity cannot be disguised as theatre for social welfare. When we read that Stuart Vaughn's New Orleans Repertory Theater is doing *Charley's Aunt,* we chuckle and say, "Whitey is doing it again." Two things happen when a play about Blacks is presented for whites (any time a play is presented on Broadway or Off-Broadway, it is presented for whites): 1) they stay away because they are not interested in the least in what Blacks are saying, because most of the time Blacks are saying some truths about the conditions in this country; or 2) whites are so conditioned by musicals and comedies and histori-cal museum pieces that they are not prepared to witness anything new.

For example, consider the recent play, *Who's Got His Own,* by Ronald Milner, at the American Place Theatre. Harold Clurman, theatre critic for *The Nation,* departed after Act I and did not review the play. Now I must point out here that *Who's Got His Own* is a Black play; American Place Theatre is a white theatre — with a good reputation. Its subscription audience is 98 percent white and, through studies, it has been proven that subscription audiences are middle class. Harold Clurman is a critic for a national magazine; he is as middle class as the audience for that play. His dismissal of *Who's Got His Own* reflects the feelings of that audience. Milner received a first-class production of his play and a second-class audience to approve its worth. The writer was caught in the paradoxical situation with which most Black artists in this

Cliff Frazier in *Lorenzacio,* New York City, 1967.

country are eventually faced: to be an American artist and at the same time to be a Negro! To please the audience, the author and the theatre would have had to lie about the Black man's condition in this country.

"The artist's function is to interpret life," says John O. Killens. "I see him as a hunter in the jungle with civilization being the jungle; his prey is truth."

Socially meaningful theatre must be truthful to the happenings of our time.

Bringing an End
to the Theft of Black Art

A BLACK WHO WORKS IN THE THEATRE, who cannot survive without it, can easily go out of his mind trying to write about it. It is even more difficult if he is a Black writer writing in a white population for a white majority. The white majority—who have unlimited access to the mass media—always expects a Black writer to prove something about the Black state of mind, something most Blacks know exist, and that whites know exist—after four major riots. Yet these same whites are trying to deny that knowledge by pretending integration is just around the corner.

In this European theatre, which is disguised as American theatre, and which is perpetuated by foundation grants, it is usually the best con men who get the money. Often they are the worst directors and administrators, because their survival depends on getting money instead of directing and administrating. Therefore, writing about the Black theatre can be a very dangerous thing. One must reveal something about the foundations as well as the con men; *because* of the foundations and the con men there is no Black theatre in this country. And, finally, I suspect the motives of the whites who claim to be interested.

Whites tell us: "We gave you the Negro Ensemble Company, The New Lafayette Theatre, Lincoln Center assignments via Diana Sands and Gloria Foster, and stardom for Sidney Poitier." But these people and institutions have nothing at all to do with Black theatre.

Let's go at it again.

The Black artist knows that if he is allowed to make a dollar from his art, some white is making ten dollars off that same piece of art.

The white theatre as it exists today is a game. Broadway is high stakes, like roulette and faro in Las Vegas. Off-Broadway is $20,000 to lose. Off-Off-Broadway is primarily alienated middle-class whites. The university theatre survives on intellectual and esoteric crap, while frowning on its starving audience two blocks away. The Black theatre is middle-class-oriented hustlers striving for acceptance in the white theatre. They are trying to get the Black experience into this game. Whites do this by laying some money on Black playwrights. (They usually accept about one every ten years.) The writer in turn, knowing his chances, pretends to reveal Black experiences to a $7.50 white audience—an audience that is running away from real experiences, away from the lifeline. And, of course, he bullshits whitey, telling him, "That's the way we really are! You ever been to Harlem, Man?" (Gettin' that money, Brother!) The $7.50-ers are being flagellated and loving it until they get home (safety), think, realize that them niggers are crazy and out for money. *Nobody—Black, green, or yellow—could be like that!* And the whites set up panel debates, questioning the Blacks. The Blacks, in turn, start "crying the blues," viz, "You don't understand us!" or "You don't really see us!" or "We are invisible!"

You see, whites have nothing to write about any more. That's why we have so many Happenings, Mixed-Media, Underground Andy Warhols: cop-outs. There was a time when they had Beaumont and Fletcher, O'Neill, Odets, Williams, Miller, and Albee. The white experience can be summed up with these writers. Any new writer is destroyed when compared. Even the educators have studied them at Yale and Northwestern. They've found the formulas and arguments to justify them. That's why European dramatists are so popular in this country. (Read the old issues of *Tulane Drama Review*.) One wonders if they really want American writers any more.

It is sad when a Black writer is compared to Albee, Miller, Williams, Odets, or O'Neill. (Can you dig a Black writer being compared to Beaumont and Fletcher?) It is sad because the Black writer is caught in the white "comparison bag." And that is usually a "form bag" that has no relation at all to the black experience. Content should always be more important than its package.

But when you are in a hurry and there are so many packages, one doesn't have the time to open all of them. The dollars move in a hurry, especially in the New York theatre. And believe this, the Black writers and performers who flock into New York from Denver, Chicago, Cleveland, Detroit, San Francisco, all come in to get some of this fame and money. (Package it right, frame it, put it on a stage, call it theatre!) If it's about Harlem and its dreams, so what? If it's about guilty whites disguised as liberals at the Broadway theatres, flagellate them!

Con men and pimps are at work. They work where there is money. There is money in New York.

Con men and pimps tell us they want to bring theatre to the Blacks. The Black community keeps telling them, "We are not going to your theatre!"

New con men and pimps with new games arrive on the scene. And they fool the Black communities "for a minute," as the pimps say. Even this can go on and on. The culturally deprived Black communities are the fools and prostitutes. And in this Black theatre game they always lose.

The Black communities have no real theatre in Harlem, Bedford-Stuyvesant, Watts, Chicago's Woodlawn, or Philadelphia's South Side.

Why must each new generation of young Black artists suffer the faults of the past generation? Why are the Black artists constantly told, "Theatre cannot work in Harlem?" Can the New Lafayette Theatre in Harlem continue without being aware of the needs of the Harlem community? Not to produce Black playwright Ed Bullins' *In the Wine Time,* but to produce Athol Fugard's *The Blood Knot* after the success of Ronald Milner's *Who's Got His Own,* becomes a crucial question among Black artists. History is being ignored; a knowledge of the people is needed. The question becomes even more crucial when Harlem finds its New Lafayette company *downtown* at the American Place Theatre. Wouldn't it have been more meaningful to produce this talent uptown first? Is it possible for an administrator to announce a three-play series and run out of money after only two plays? Also, not to produce LeRoi Jones at this time in our history stops any theatre from being a truly Black theatre. The question becomes: does Harlem need a non-Black theatre?

The New Lafayette Theatre burned down on January 31, 1968. Three days earlier, Robert Macbeth, the director, had given permission to the *Onyx Magazine* staff for use of the facilities for that day. The occasion: a book party for one of the most important yet controversial books ever written by a Black writer, *The Crisis of the Negro Intellectual* by Harold Cruse. On hand to discuss the book were Roy Innis, Larry Neal, Preston Wilcox, Bill Strickland, Sylvester Leakes, and Charlie Russell. This panel attracted both militant and middle-class Blacks to the theatre. The New Lafayette took on a new identity in Harlem; it became a necessity. The fact that it was a theatre became secondary. The community showed that it needed first a cultural center, a meeting place, to discuss its art, its politics, and its economics. Because of the importance of New Lafayette's new direction, many Blacks in the Harlem community are questioning whether the fire was accidental.

In Watts, at Douglass House, a fine Black theatre could be developed; writers have gathered there to voice their anger about a Black community which is home. They are spokesmen for the Black community and in addition they are grassroot Black artists. In Chicago, the Blackstone Rangers found the key. Collectively they brought together the highly successful *Opportunity,*

Please Knock. The Free Southern Theatre, founded by John O'Neal and Gilbert Moses, seems to be making meaningful strides in taking theatres to Blacks in the South. However, the plays that are presented in Mississippi, Louisiana, Georgia, Tennessee, and parts of Alabama are mostly by white writers such as Brecht, Beckett, and Duberman. O'Neal and company came to New York in 1965 to raise funds and presented *Waiting for Godot* in white face. It was praised by the *Village Voice.* John O'Neal and Gilbert Moses haven't been South since that time. Tom Dent is handling the directorship of Free Southern Theatre. Yet we haven't heard too much about Free Southern Theatre since it received a Rockefeller Grant in early 1967.

O'Neal began "alternative service" shortly after the New York performances. As a conscientious objector he was assigned work first in a children's home and later with the Committee for Racial Justice of the National Council of Churches. He has remained very active with the FST, making frequent trips to New Orleans and supervising the FST's funding and administrative operations in New York. Gil Moses remained with the FST throughout the 1965 season, serving for a time as artistic director of the company. He toured with the FST during the summer of 1965, performing in *The Rifles of Senora Carrar* and *In White America,* which was revived for the 1965 tour. Moses left the FST in March 1966, after a long series of debates on the "Black-white" issue. Moses argued for an all-Black theatre, and his idea was supported by most of those in the FST. He left the theatre for personal reasons. His play, *Roots,* was performed by the FST during the 1966 season. Tom Dent took over the New Orleans leadership of the theatre in 1966. O'Neal plans to return permanently to the South and the FST as soon as his alternative service is over. Moses is presently writing, arranging, playing, and singing his own music in New York and Boston.

But Black writers, not Beckett and Duberman, should be speaking to these southern Black communities.

There is no need for the Theatre of Living Arts to be in the South Side of Philadelphia except, of course, less rent for the theatre. I feel the same way about Society Hill Playhouse in the same area in South Philadelphia. These theatres serve no purpose for the community around them. The same holds true for the Negro Ensemble Company, which is located in the Second Avenue Jewish community on New York's Lower East Side, historically known for its Jewish theatres. Is there a need to cultivate the Jewish community? To perpetuate Jewish Nationalism?

Robert Hooks, the talented young producer, co-founder with Barbara Ann Teer of the Group Theatre Workshop, predecessor of the Negro Ensemble Company, is responsible for all sixty young Black performers having jobs and professional training. He wanted the youngsters of the Group Theatre Workshop to have a company to grow into. A company where they could eventually be paid. And it did not really matter where. His apartment was too small for sixty students. He unsuccessfully sought permanent space for the Group Theatre Workshop. His last place of action was the St. Mark's Playhouse with the Ward plays, *Day of Absence* and *Happy Ending.* If he had produced them in a Harlem theatre, he would have selected that theatre, when the Ford grant came through. I don't really think he thought beyond that. The Group Theatre Workshop had been asking for money for a long time. They did Barbara Ann Teer's production of *We Real Cool.* It was a hit. Mr. Hook's production of the two Ward plays hit. The money came.

It might not have been Douglas Turner Ward's and Robert Hook's intention to begin in Harlem, but certainly they must soon move there. It will be in Harlem that our best playwrights—Lonnie Elder, LeRoi Jones, Ed Bullins, Ronald Milner, George Bass, Clifford Mason, Douglas Turner Ward and other Black writers will be appreciated. The Negro Ensemble and the New Lafayette Theatre—because of their position now as spokesmen for Black theatres, as well as for Black communities—will have to deal with Black playwrights. If they cannot deal with these writers, they must eventually cease to speak or seek grants for "Black community theatre." They must seek them for Robert Macbeth and Douglas Turner Ward.

At the January 1968, Drama Desk held at Sardi's (West), the Blacks were called to talk to the white press on "Integration or Separation for Negroes in American Theatre?" On the panel were Godfrey Cambridge, Diana Sands, Josephine Premice, Bernard Gersten, Robert Macbeth, and Douglas Turner Ward. Of these panelists, Mr. Ward is most important, because the Negro Ensemble Company represents the Black community's single most important possibility. Mr. Ward himself bridges Black thought from the late forties to the sixties. He is a brilliant writer, excellent actor, and more than competent stage director. But he is not fully aware of the ascendancy of Black consciousness that reached unparalleled heights in 1965. At this panel Mr. Ward stated, according to *Show Business:* "There is no ideological reason for a Black theatre, Negro audiences are tougher, as anyone who played the Apollo in Harlem would know—if a Black audience is bored, they go to sleep. The idea of a separate Negro audience is not new. Earlier aborted enterprises were the American Negro Theatre and The Manhattan Arts Theatre." Should Blacks go to sleep if the play is white-oriented or directed away from them? As a matter of fact, they should walk out. The Manhattan Arts Theatre and the American Negro Theatre were products of the late forties.

The author of the article in *Show Business,* Thomas R. Dash, gave his views on the panel: "From 1900 until about 1940, the Yiddish Theatre on the East Side flourished and produced Kessler, Adler, Maurice Schwartz, and Boris Thomashensky, to name just a few. As the second generation of Jews began to be assimilated, many went over to the American theatre. The Jews produced great playwrights (Arthur Miller), great producers (Merrick, Gordon, Shumlin, and Alex Cohen), great designers, and great actors and comedians. Paul Muni actually started on the Jewish stage. This ethnic experience proved without a doubt that you can have both Separatist Theatre and Integrated Theatre."

Blacks do have non-professional theatres in Newark and Detroit. The Spirit House in Newark is there because LeRoi Jones had the thoughts and power to *make* one, after he proved to the young Black artists in that city that he had the power and stamina to endure. By helping this theatre, the foundations could prove for once to be what they pretend to be about: perpetuating American art and American artists.

In another area, the Concept-East Theatre in Detroit, also non-professional, came out of a basic need. Specifically, Black artists had tried integrating the white theatres. That didn't work. So, we started our own theatre. The reasons were very basic (most things in the theatre are basic): We did not intend to put any more time into the small, biased white community theatres, time usually spent painting sets or playing small "buddy roles." We wanted to play lead roles, have a say in what plays would be done, and be directors of some plays. Whitey told us to go to hell.

Again, *we started our own thing.* Basic but not simple, even though it should have been. Whites began to talk about us, write about us, even question our ability as artists. Under all of this, they of course, in these debates and writings, made some money off us. And the more we withdrew, the more valuable the information about us became.

Now, however, years later, I realize that secretly Concept-East artists wanted to take the cute little theatres away from the whites but at the time didn't know enough about the technical end of theatre. But the Black artists had more to say organically even if they did not have the technique to say it. After they found all that came from getting out there doing it, the whites were no longer necessary. Still, while there, the Blacks were nice, clean, articulate. Most of them pretended they were interested in that avant-garde bullshit. (Similarly a few Blacks now are pretending they are interested in the psychedelic and folk rock movement in the Village.) The white theatres as usual relegated them to the back. *They started their own thing.*

Was it their own thing or the Black community's own thing?

It took the Concept-East a whole season to find their thing was not revivals of Broadway and Off-Broadway plays with Black casts. But they did find their groove. That's important. Concept-East arrived at this point of its destination after almost five years of driving. And we know how we got there. We read the signs, marked the trees, and even left a chalk line. *We know*.

It took Concept-East two years to communicate with the community. (Isn't that what a Black theatre in a Black community is supposed to be about? Communication?) The artists at the Concept had withdrawn so far from the people in the community they did not know how to deal with the winos and prostitutes. When they tried to come to the theatre, when they asked: "Is this a bar?" "Is this a church?" "What time is the service?" we ran them away. It was because we wanted to keep the few "middle-class" Blacks that filled about ten seats safe from them.

We even journeyed miles out of the community trying to get those doctors, lawyers, and chiefs. But when the artists learned to deal with the community, Concept-East began to live. The plays and their productions took on new and exciting form.

At this point in our history, who could start a meaningful Black theatre in the various sections of the country? Dick Gregory could make a theatre in Chicago's Woodlawn community. Douglas Turner Ward could maintain a theatre in Harlem. At present, CORE, Urban League, NAACP, Muslims or the Baptist Church could sustain a National Black Theatre. Will they?

Again, there is nothing to prove. Theatre is basic. Black theatre has nothing at all to do with a collection of writings by Beckett, Shakespeare, Broadway, Cafe La Mama, Walter Kerr, Pinter, Actors' Equity, Ford Foundation, Yale School of Drama. . . . *We know there is nothing to prove.* And if you think Black artists are going to waste that precious time and energy, you won't know what I'm talking about. The places and names mentioned are ways to publicity (and in some cases money) for Black actors and writers. Money is what the white majority understands. And as Langston Hughes writes: *Money and art are far apart.*

A majority of the young Black artists are fed up with the way white people are stealing Black art. They are very angry with the Black pimps and hustlers. Some see no hope and slash their wrists, thus ending it all. A few stopped talking a long time ago. They stare. Sometimes they smile simply like inmates in an asylum. Some bullshit whitey, as I said earlier, "Makin' that moonn-neee, brother!" —talking faster than whitey can listen.

However, a new crop of young Black artists is coming onto the scene. They come via the poverty programs from the Black ghettos. Theirs is a true

Leonard Jackson (middle) and Anna Horosford in "Great Goodness of Life—A Coon Show" from *A Black Quartet*, New York, 1969.

Black art because they came of age in the segregated sixties. The foundation grant doesn't mean anything because they've received them—along with the problems they bring—under the poverty programs.

Now, in 1968, with the ascendancy of Black consciousness, these artists are valuable because they had withdrawn so far their own people couldn't find them. Since this withdrawal was indirect, they want to return and speak to the Black masses. (Maybe even to the young Black and white college students who in the last couple of years were caught in the chaos of the Black revolution.) The Black artists want to talk to them because it looks as if they will be the ones inheriting the stocks and real estate.

Perhaps this is what it's all about.

Langston's Leaving Never Meant He Was Gone

IT MUST HAVE BEEN TWO OR three years after high school, or at least two or three years before college—there was a five-year gap for me—that I found Langston Hughes. I didn't find him in high school or college. In the high school that I attended, especially the American literature classes, Black writers were foreign, Black poets were nonexistent. In my college they were ignored. During the fifties, when I came of age, discovering, searching, groping for identification, teachers often turned me on to Robert Lowell, Vachel Lindsay, Eugene O'Neill, William Faulkner, Robert Penn Warren, Mark Twain, Henry James, Hart Crane, and, of course, Ernest Hemingway. They were described as "true American writers" because they were white, born here, or wrote here. There was no labelling of Langston Hughes as "American" because, in his poetry and prose, there is a deep and abiding love for this country as well as for the Black man in this country.

I found Langston Hughes during my intense study of the Black theatre (I discovered theatre in the five-year gap, too). Dr. Alain Locke discussed Black writers in the collection, *Thirteen Plays for the Negro Theater*. It is one of the earliest published anthologies of plays about Black life-styles. (I wish I could find that book.) He mentioned how Langston's plays had received praise at the Karamu House Theatre in Cleveland. Langston led me to other Black writers, Black institutions. He led me to Richard Wright, *Crisis* magazine, James Baldwin, Ralph Ellison, W.C. Handy, *Mercury* magazine . . . even to Carl Van Vechten. . . . From articles and books I found that Langston was a poet, short story writer, translator and adaptor. I exhausted myself in the library reading Langston Hughes: "Soul Gone Home," at least ten times; "A Good Job Done," fifteen times; "Early Autumn," one of the most beautiful short stories in American letters, two or three dozen times. Poems: "Weary Blues," "A House in Taos" to "I've Known Rivers," "Montage of a dream deferred. . . ."

So, I was aware of him long before I met him. Similarly, I am aware of God, of Pushkin; if only I could have met *them*!

It was 1961. The newspaper, the *Negro* newspaper, announced that Langston Hughes would be coming to Detroit, given the key to the city, and would be escorted from the airport by police motorcade downtown to the City Council Building. Our new city chief, Mayor Jerome P. Cavanagh, would then present the poet with the key to Detroit!

On the afternoon of the following day, after Langston had received the key, Ronald Milner, a writer friend, called me. He had met Langston and *he* had impressed Langston. My friend wanted me to go with him that very afternoon and meet Langston Hughes.

"Are you available, man?" he asked.

Langston was staying at the Park-Shelton in the art center section of Detroit. Equidistance from everything: downtown, westside, eastside...

It seemed that all my "artsy-craftsy" friends knew him, yet before the Negro press announced his arrival I assumed no one knew him because no one ever mentioned him or his work. However, he was a celebrity among the Blacks, i.e., the factory workers, the car washers, the day workers, domestics, bartenders.... They knew *one* of his poems or *one* of his short stories or *one* of his plays or *some* of *Simple* they had read in the Chicago *Defender*.

Margaret Danner, the poet, and a dear friend to Detroit artists and writers, had introduced Ronald to Langston. So, naturally, respect and aspiration for Langston grew because I knew then that the man had to be real. One can determine the effect of a man by the ones who love him, so it was with Langston Hughes before I met him.

At about that time, we were involved in something in Detroit called, for nothing better, Black Discovery. We had built our own theatre, called Concept-East; Margaret Danner had opened Boone House for poets; Henri King had opened the Contemporary Art Gallery; and both Tony Brown and Richard Henry (Brother Imari) started publishing little magazines. We had a lot of things to talk to Langston about. Would he listen? Had the new mayor and the middle-class Negro doctors and lawyers cornered him on this Detroit visit?

The first thing he did on my arrival at the hotel was to offer me a drink. I refused (I don't drink! *What? A writer and director? Don't drink?*). Then he smiled. The cigarette with the ashes not falling sort of blocking some of the smile. How can I describe that smile? Have you ever studied the Mona Lisa? Draw in a cigarette with ashes. Langston's smile would create the same effect. He told us how swinging the suite was: *Man, I wish I had one of these permanently. This is something, isn't it? Wow! Hey, they gave me the key to the city.* (He started looking for the key but evidently had misplaced it.) *Brought me in by motorcade! I wish I had the money they spent on me!*

And we all broke up laughing. He was real.

Later that evening he spoke for Arthur Coar, local director for the Association for the Study of Negro Life and History, the organization founded in the twenties by Carter Wodson, also one of the first men to hire Langston.

He and I talked again that night. I told him how much I liked his short story, "Early Autumn." He told me to look him up if I came to New York. I talked of the conditions of the Black man in the theatre. I do remember he gave Ronald Milner a copy of his plays, *Don't You Want To Be Free?* and *Soul Gone Home.* And we tried to get a cast together to do a reading of his poetry and the two plays. But he left two days later before we could get the actors. Parting, he said something like, *It's kinda hard to get colored people together, but once you got them . . . well. . . .* And he smiled that smile preoccupied with his packing.

In early 1964, I moved to New York. (I found the opportunity via Rev. Malcolm Boyd and his play, *Study in Color.*) I called Langston after about a week of the cruelties of New York City.

"Hi Woodie," he said, "come on over. How is Ron? Did he finish that big book?"

He lived in Harlem on 127th Street in one of those beautiful brownstones. I had trouble finding the house. I searched around and finally I asked a policeman. "Yeah, the poet. He lives in the next block." His office was on the third floor. It was filled with books by Black writers—fiction and non-fiction from Blacks the world over. Most of the books had some personal identification for him because Langston had helped in getting them published or had written the introduction or had helped the writer when the writer was beginning. The first thing he said, "I read that story, 'Beautiful Light and Black Our Dreams,' in *Negro Digest.* It's good." I didn't know how to respond. I do remember there was a long pause. He did not fill the pause. He made me fill it. I started explaining the story, gaining confidence as I talked. Suddenly, I realized that we were talking man to man, not student to teacher or student to Great Artist. We talked about the works of other writers, particularly Ron Milner ("That big, big book—Is it really going to be 1,500 pages?"), Malraux, Ellison, Sandburg, Whitman, Wright, and Dostoevsky. I found he never talked about his work. Instead, he gave me copies of his book, including the autobiography, *The Big Sea,* autographing it in large bold green ink strokes, "Especially for Woodie King—with a hearty welcome to New York. Sincerely, Langston Hughes, Harlem, U.S.A., April 1964."

On my leaving, he invited me down to the Greenwich Mews Theatre's sanctuary to see his play, *Jericho—Jim Crow.* In that brief visit, Langston

Hughes, as he must have done with many other Black artists, opened himself and thus accepted me and listened to me. I don't think I had talked to any artist as I talked to him. Yet the meeting was brief, less than two hours. But this is a long time for a busy writer.

Within the next year, we met often. He invited me to other plays, recommended me for parts. I even read for his play, *Prodigal Son*.

In October of 1965, I invited him to the opening of Ron Milner's *Who's Got His Own?* at American Place Theatre. I was directing it as a work-in-progress. He was eager to see Milner's play. He liked its construction but he felt "that boy, Tim, Jr. is awfully mad, they better not put a white character on stage talking about Negroes that way, they'll get picketed."

Our next meeting was in Cleveland at Karamu Playhouse's Golden Anniversary. I had been invited out by the theater department. I didn't know Langston would be there but I did know they would be doing his play, *Simply Heavenly.* As fate would have it, we all stayed in the same hotel and, since it was some distance from the playhouse, we shared a cab (Langston, Malcolm Boyd, Fredrick O'Neal, Sidney Lanier).

"It's something of an event to have Langston back," Rowena Jelliffe remarked on the opening panel. "Langston Hughes was Karamu's first playwright away back when it supported the Gilpin Players." His play, *Little Mam,* received wide acclaim at the Karamu Playhouse. On the panel discussion that included the above-mentioned participants, he did not put anyone down. He praised LeRoi Jones as one of the finest young writers in the theatre. He felt LeRoi Jones was equal to the best of the 20th-century poets. At this point, LeRoi was catching hell from the white press because of his Black Arts Repertory Theatre.

While we were in Cleveland talking about theatre, New York was in the midst of the now famous blackout. Most of the New Yorkers decided to remain an extra day in Cleveland until it was over. Thus I had an opportunity to continue my dialogue with Langston about poetry and the blues; we had certainly talked about it enough, so much that I thought he was bored with it. I told him what I wanted to do: take his first book of poetry, *The Weary Blues,* adapt it to the stage, using the prose and poetry from that first book to his last, set it in Harlem, and add W.C. Handy's blues as an integral part since he and Handy were saying the same things. He liked the idea, the possibilities. He even gave me a few more copies of his work. The idea would be to follow a young Black American from a storefront church through the Harlem streets and finally to the foreign soil of some distant land. An American soldier protecting this country from . . . his death.

The Cleveland visit brought Langston and me even closer, if only for a fleeting moment. Now I would be able to adapt his work with his consent and his help. For two months I worked off and on with him. We agreed that no corrections would be made until I finished a first draft.

In March of 1966, I gave him a third and final draft of my adaptation of *The Weary Blues*. He made large bold corrections and additions in the characteristic green ink and returned it to me in April. I went to his home again to pick it up.

"You did it," he said.

"Yes, it took a lot of research," I said. "Man, you got work in Schomburg nobody ever heard of since 1934. I wanted to use something from the old *Mercury* and *Opportunity* magazines."

"I didn't want you to use any piece that was dated; that's the only thing I was afraid of," he said. "People find the skeletons in your closet, they don't understand, they get uptight."

I knew exactly what he meant. I had been tempted to adapt a huge full-length play. Between the Countee Cullen Library and the Schomburg collection I compiled enough material for a dozen full-length plays. When I started cutting material from the Scottsboro Boys as it appeared in *Theater News,* a piece that was good and fitted *Weary,* but outdated, I knew I had found a spine for the play. Agitprop theatre of the thirties did not fit the theme we had set for *The Weary Blues.*

He gave me his corrected copy of *The Weary Blues:* with it were seven new poems that he felt should be included, plus a new play, *Mother and Child* (I directed it at The American Place Theatre about a month later while he was in Dakar). He had marked the script appropriately, large green arrows indicated where the new additions should be placed. Then it was off to Dakar for the First World Festival of Negro Art for Langston.

He sent me a postcard. Then, in August, he called to let me know he was back in New York for a minute. "What's happening with *Weary Blues?*"

"Good news! We have a production at the Lincoln Center Museum and Library series sponsored by Equity Library Theatre."

The Weary Blues opened at the Lincoln Center in October of 1966 for a limited engagement. It was packed every night. Langston was there almost every night. He would give a little chuckle every night because I had Mississippi John Hurt's "Got The Blues and Can't Be Satisfied" at full volume to put the audience in the right mood before the play. He brought a lot of Black guests. He also helped cast the play by securing the services of Miss Theresa Merritt.

I remember, after the performance, the actor Robert Hooks invited us to his apartment for drinks. It was a lively evening. And as I remember it, Langston only stayed a minute. But he did want to come by to tell all the young performers how much he enjoyed the play and the direction in which we had taken his prose and poetry. He was especially pleased with Eleo Pomare's beautiful junkie dance and Norma Bush's Preacher and Cliff Frazier's Hustler. It was a strange evening. After Langston left, we spent the remainder of the evening quoting and reciting his poetry. You see, Langston's leaving never meant that he was gone. He always left something behind for the Black people.

He was always busy. He had a lot of things going, works not yet completed, publishers after overdue manuscripts. I always dreaded the thought of dropping in on him. I would often wait until Ronald Milner came into New York so that we could both spring ideas, which always meant a long and rewarding evening for me. In December of 1966, his secretary, novelist Lindsey Patterson, called and told me that Langston Hughes was busy but that he wanted to compile a book of short stories for Little Brown and Company. Did I have anything? Of course! I sent him the story that he liked from *Negro Digest,* "Beautiful Light and Black Our Dreams." He liked it and published it in the anthology, *Best Short Stories by Negro Writers.*

I ran into him a month later in January of 1965, in a small Village restaurant, after a performance of *Day of Absence* and *Happy Ending*. It was one of those cold evenings, threatening rain. I don't remember exactly what we talked about. I do know I had given a friend who was starting a magazine Langston's private telephone number and I was afraid he would not approve of it. He was annoyed about it. I told him I had tried to reach him by phone to tell him he would get this call but that his researcher, Raoul Abdul, told me he was out. He was with friends in the restaurant so we didn't talk much. I thought he would never talk to me again. I told him I would call him but he said he would be away until the middle of February and would call me when he returned.

He did call.

He wanted me to adapt his collection on Jesse B. Simple to the stage! "Are you interested? Drop by this evening, old boy. We have a producer for the fall season."

I remember standing in his library saying, for lack of anything better, "Man . . . man!" He knew I knew the work because of the earlier research on *The Weary Blues.* He wanted to give me original material, from the first Chicago *Defender* article to the final New York *Post* article. In addition, he wanted to know if I could do it by June because the producers, Stella Holt and

Francis Durcker, would have to read it. He also told me they had Alvin Ailey set to direct it. I remember telling him it would be ready by the middle of May.

After reading the material again, I told him what I wanted the character to cover, the time of action, and of course the place, Harlem, U.S.A. We both got excited talking about what should be done with Simple: it would be set in the night since the Black ghetto usually comes alive after dark. Simple would be allowed to move freely in the chaos of existence. He would desperately search for some order in this chaos; always explaining, searching, hoping in Langston Hughes's dialogue, Langston Hughes's poetry, showing how "White folk is the cause of a lot of inconvenience in my life," how they steal pieces of him, how his moral and religious faith in others save him from total destruction.

I finished the play, *Simple's Blues*, on April 3, 1967. Langston called me April 13, 1967, from the Hotel Wellington. At the time, he was working on a project for Harry Belafonte. He moved into the Wellington because, there, he could get away from the phone. It also gave him a chance to read the play immediately. He liked the play but felt it had too many characters. It would cost over $15,000; the producer had only $20,000 for the two plays, *Ask Your Mama* and *Simple's Blues*.

We had some cheese dip. He and Raoul Abdul had wine with theirs and ordered me Coke. I suggested that he should eat better. We laughed; we felt we had a hit if Stella Holt found the extra money or if I found a way to "cut some of those people out." I understood what he was indirectly telling me and went to work on the rewrites. I finished them on May 6, 1967. I called Langston immediately. He was in the hospital. He died May 22, 1967.

Langston Hughes (left), Vinnette Carroll, and Ralph Bunche, New York City.

We Must Break
with European Traditions

IF THE AMERICAN THEATRE
isn't really the American theatre, how can Black Theatre in America be
anything but a Black artist's dream. "Black Theatre" is a term that says where
Blacks in this nonexistent American theatre would like to go—not where they
are. No real American form has emerged in this country's short history. In the
late twenties when Eugene O'Neill and the Provincetown group tried to do
new and vital work, that one percent that make up the theatre-going audience
retreated with shock. However, in the thirties, O'Neill was joined by Clifford
Odets, Irwin Shaw, Sidney Kingsley, Maxwell Anderson, and Paul Green,
and the country thought it had finally found an American theatre. Unfortunately, it had not. It had only succeeded in producing an American August
Strindburg via O'Neill and different forms of Russian literature via Odets,
Anderson and their contemporaries. The crossing of contemporary American
ethnic with traditional European theatre seemed to be the American way.
America had taken what seemed to be the best of Europe. However, what
seemed to be the best emerged as the cover of a very complicated book.

In terms of physical structure, theatres are still, to this day, of the pros-
cenium type used all over Europe. These theatres were designed for operas
from their inception. Every new stage design is based on an earlier European
design discovered by careful research. Plays are written to fit into something
similar to a box. This makes most of the plays identical. Plays written in the
thirties were presented in boxes. American plays cannot be restricted by
theatres designed for European opera. Paul Green, who worked with the
Stanislavski-oriented Group Theater in the Group's beginning and who was an
innovator in pioneering Black drama in America—*White Dresses, In
Abraham's Bosom, Native Son, Hymn to the Rising Sun*—moved to outdoor
symphonic form (he went back to him home in North Carolina and again
pioneered one of the few true American forms in symphonic drama). O'Neill,
who experimented with Black plays—*The Dreamy Kid, The Emperor Jones,*

The Slave cast, New York City, 1965-66, starring Al Freeman, Jr.

All God's Chillun Got Wings —moved deeper into his own family and emerged as one of the finest American playwrights and the only one to win the Nobel Prize.

The plays about Blacks written by these white men were viewed by a white audience. That's how they were meant to be viewed. No attempt to change this pattern occurred until the mid-fifties after the demise of the "Negro Theatres" in Harlem and the fashionable "night out" in Harlem became unfashionable. It was about that time that a series of small community projects discovered that survival meant developing within the community. Actors who had worked with the white groups were instrumental in developing Black community groups. In New York it was Rose McClendon, Frank Wilson, Fred O'Neal; in Chicago it was Ted Ward; in Cleveland it was Charles Gilpin. The *community* naturally meant among Black peers. Gradually the plays changed from revivals of white plays with all-Black casts to original dramas written by writers familiar with the Black life-style. The plays no longer were written for white acceptance since no white people would see them. In schools, YMCAs, churches —across the country, from Los Angeles' Watts to New York's Harlem —plays tried to communicate to those nearest, those next door. This was done out of necessity, out of a need to survive. The audiences were few but they responded. More Blacks tried their hand at playwriting.

In the thirties and forties the Communists tried to use theatre; in the fifties the politicians tried to use theatre; in the sixties social workers tried to use theatre. Theatre communicated directly and quickly. There was no way easier or cheaper to reach Black people. Then, in the late fifties, Lorraine Hansberry's *Raisin in the Sun* hit. *Raisin* reaffirmed in Blacks the necessity for more involvement in Black theatre. As a matter of fact, Lonnie Elder III, Robert Hooks, Douglas Turner Ward and Ossie Davis were all in *Raisin in the Sun.* Until the late fifties no Black writer, Black actor, Black director or technician had benefited financially from any of the plays about Black people which had been presented in years previous. It had always been a white writer who had profited. Phillip Yordan's *Anna Lucasta* is a case in point. Marc Connelly's *Green Pastures, Porgy and Bess, In Abraham's Bosom* ...on down the line ...are all cases in point.

The years 1959, 1960, and 1961 marked the beginning of the coffee house theatre in New York. The so-called avant-garde. The outcast theatres: Cafe Cino, Cafe La Mama, and the hang-outs of the Beat Generation. Blacks were accepted in this circle because the circle itself was about freedom —the destruction of The System.

In the early sixties, the poverty programs around the country came into existence. Social workers tried to use theatre, and young people who had only dreamed of participating in the theatre arts now had the opportunity to participate through so-called cultural-enrichment programs. Towards the mid-sixties these projects became more serious. The message became the medium. Serious Black writers submitted their plays after realizing that the plays wouldn't be done in the mainstream theatres. The underground flocked to see productions of these writers. The writers received major attention from the same critics who reviewed plays on Broadway and Off-Broadway.

Street theatre and guerilla theatre emerged as forerunners of Black theatre. Street theatre *takes* theatre directly to the people who cannot afford to *go* to the theatre. Phoebe Brand, director of Theater in the Street, was the first to make an attempt. She discovered almost immediately that for people in the inner city to relate, performers had to be multi-racial. It became impossible for Theater in the Street to present its repertory in English alone. Spanish communities insisted that plays presented in their community communicate to them in their language. Guerilla theatre is an attempt at agitprop theatre. It attacks the government in general and the injustices of war in particular. Both forms used Black people to help solve problems that were not directly related to the immediate needs of Black people.

Young Blacks dissatisfied with the poverty program structure moved out on their own and set up their own thing. This was true of the New Lafayette Theatre. This theatre had been a part of Harlem Youth Unlimited. New Lafayette Theatre's director, Robert Macbeth, had a vision that went beyond the limited idea of Haryou's federal project. Macbeth wanted a theatre controlled exclusively by Black people, free to experiment within Black culture, free to try new forms — the same freedom that Black Americans fought for in all the other areas of their existence. This could hardly happen within a federally supported project. The New Lafayette Theatre moved into its new quarters at the old Elk hall in 1965 and Macbeth started to build what he believes to be a Black theatre. The foundation of this theatre must be the community around it. "The classic function of the theatre is to project and illuminate the feelings and concerns of the community which sustains it. Thus, the theatre, like the church, is a community ritual." And Black theatre cannot emerge, until it is free of the European concept, *"until we change our language, yeah. As we won't be free until we change our music, or we won't be free until we change our theatre; until we begin to do the rituals again, when we start doing the rituals again and stop doing 'plays'."*

The New Lafayette Theatre is a theatre that can become a Black Theatre.

When it is no longer supported by foundations, when it has to exist because the Black people of Harlem want it, it will be Black. The New Lafayette Theatre, in its four years, came into its own when Ed Bullins, the young Black writer from Philadelphia via San Francisco journeyed to the New Lafayette. He brought with him a collection of plays that were written for Black people. They are so directed for Black ears that whites reading them learn more about Black culture than do the Blacks to whom the plays are directed. However, there is little doubt of Bullins' direction. Unlike many Black writers who exist without benefit of a permanent company, Bullins writes, knowing that his plays will be performed. His position is very similar to that of O'Neill and Odets. O'Neill had the Provincetown Company to test his plays and Odets had the Group Theater. Odets also had Harold Clurman and Elia Kazan, as well as some of the finest trained performers outside of the Moscow Art Theatre. Bullins has the possibilities of a similar playwright-company relationship.

But it is important that we understand the difference between a Black Eugene O'Neill and a true Black playwright. *At this time* there can be no Black theatre unless it is a free theatre or a cooperative effort by all involved. Whenever money enters into the picture it is best to treat theatre as a business. Unfortunately, most of the Black people who are active in theatre, or those on the sidelines hoping to jump into theatre, should be treated precisely as one would treat a white boy. There is a magic which theatre images project in the minds of Black writers and Black performers. They don't see *theatre* as ever having been fair to them. And they are absolutely correct. An art form that is unfair to white people is twice as unfair to the few Black people who try to crack it. A $25,000 play produced by foundation support in a Black community and playing to no Black people is the same as a $25,000 play produced by limited partnership Off-Broadway playing to white people. In both cases it's the audience that determines the play's validity.

To the performer and writer, the Negro Ensemble Company is *no different than the American Place Theatre is no different than the New Lafayette Theatre*. Before a company of performers come together they are individual in their thinking and in their actions. One thinks of oneself before he thinks of the collective. And since everything about him is the same as the things away from him, his thoughts usually remain the way they were when he entered the new surroundings. By way of elaboration, The Last Poets and LeRoi Jones's Spirit House Movers are projections of new thoughts and fresh attempts at form because they are not confined by time and space. Real estate is not important. European concepts are not attempted. Their form of presentation goes back to "Early American" form, i.e., to the minstrel shows, blues, spirituals, even in many cases to moans and screams. In LeRoi Jones' case, he learned the European forms early and therefore learned early how meaningless they are to the expression of the Black life-style. On the other hand, the Last Poets never learned European forms at all. They found their form in Black music and from Black musicians. The American Black actor doesn't have the proper frame of reference. His is a European concept. It is basically the same with the Black playwright. He is less than three decades out of the European tradition. Whether he is with the Negro Ensemble Company, the American Place Theatre or the New Lafayette Theatre, his frame of reference and his form will be the same. Breaking that tradition might be what James Brown, the Muslims, Smokey Robinson and Rev. C.L. Franklin are doing. Theirs might be the real Black "theatre." Whatever, it must be a bitch being artistic director in a theatre where twenty-five Blacks, Negroes and colored people are all together.

The audiences that attend plays written and performed by Black artists are usually of three types: whites who want to be flagellated; liberals who either want their fears confirmed or those who want to steal the art; and the few Blacks who go hoping that it will be good because Blacks are involved. For those who want to get flagellated there are all those horrible "get whitey" plays that are usually written directly to white people, ignoring Black people completely. These plays are meaningless. No one with any knowledge at all believes what's happening on stage. The liberals are in another bag. They are not interested at all in the real play, the real theatre. They want the Moynihan Report confirmed, all those reports from the Welfare Department verified. If all this happens, then intellectual discussion can be set. Nothing will happen as a result of these debates. One or two Black intellectuals who almost always are invited and who always start the discussion by stating that they haven't seen the play but. . . . You know these intellectuals well. They all got their jobs because the Black Nationalists raised a lot of hell. And finally, the Black audience is just happy to see something Black on stage. They are not excited by reviews. They want it real. "Tell it like it is!" They are only a few, and they are mostly students, and it's usually very difficult for them to get to the theatre. This is the audience that Black writers try to speak to. However, theatre economics are twenty years ahead of them when it should be equal to them.

And so it came to pass—the day Black artists realized they would never be accepted in the mainstream of American life. It came very early in theatre. It was (and still is) the nut that few Blacks are able to crack. This is due to the direct and immediate image projected. LeRoi Jones called it Revolutionary Theatre: "The plays that will split the heavens for us will be called 'the destruction of America.' The heroes will be Crazy Horse, Denmark Vesey, Patrice Lumumba, but not history, not memory, not sad sentimental groping for a warmth in our despair.'' It was an art that had to express in beautiful and artistic form the life-style of its participants. Black participants wanted to create their own Othellos, their own Willy Lomans. This came, too, when the country, as its artists, was (and still is) going through terrible changes, political and social. After 360 years Blacks can no longer believe anything white people say and are indeed making them face up to their lies. Nothing short of death could force the Blacks to be Negroes.

Black theatre cannot survive under the present conditions. Black performers and black technicians cannot invest it with the same rules and regulations that characterize white theatre. It's like telling a child that he is a man. As Vantile Whitfield, director of the Performing Arts Society of Los Angeles (PASLA) informed us, ''Black theatre is embryonic.''

Black theatre is about the destruction of tradition. Listen to Ronald Milner, playwright and director of Spirit of Shango Theater in Detroit, run it down: ''It will be a theatre having to do with love of one's self, and one's personal, national and international family; with wariness and hatred of one's personal, national and international enemies; with, ideally, points as to how to break their grip and splatter their power.''

It exists to make way for Black thought and Black artistic expression. Ideally, it should be in a Black community. It cannot be directly supported by a foundation! But an audience-development program can be supported. It must be supported by the people of the particular audience it reaches out to. Audience-development drives similar to voter-registration drives should be supported by foundations. Just as young workers ventured into Black communities to encourage Black people to vote, the effort to get them to subscribe to a Black theatre of their choice should be attempted. It doesn't matter whether that audience is Black or white. Ideally, it should direct itself to Black people. Most whites are aware that Black theatre is for Black audiences and that's why so few attend real Black theatre. They don't really want to know what it's all about. They want you to be lied to or to be flagellated. They don't want Black theatre to talk to and try to teach Blacks. That would mean that Blacks would be shown who their enemy is. Anyone who has attended over three plays knows what will sell to Broadway, Off-Broadway, and Off-Off-Broadway. That's not the problem. The problem is: what does one present to Black people to encourage them to pack a church, to enjoy themselves in their favorite tavern, to wait in line to get in the Apollo, to buy three rock 'n' roll albums by Soul Brother Number One week after week, and to go to see *Hello Dolly!* and *The Great White Hope* and all kinds of commercial theatre?

As Ed Bullins puts it, "If the Black community were organized to support its Black artists, they would not have to feel fortunate and beholding to rich white people to get their theatre going. There is enough money in Black America to support all of the Black arts and the new Black cultural groups springing up among our youth. If every Black Cadillac driver missed one payment and sent it to a Black theatre in his community, or near him, this would be achieved. If every showcase Black millionaire gave $10,000 yearly to a National Black Arts Foundation, this goal of Black community support for Black arts would become a reality. And the money is tax deductible."

At this point, I would like to go a little into *A Black Quartet,* four one-act plays by Ed Bullins, Ben Caldwell, LeRoi Jones, and Ronald Milner. The four plays were done first at Chelsea Theater Center in the Bedford-Stuyvesant section of Brooklyn. They were moved Off-Broadway in July 1969 to the Gate Theater in the Village. Money for the production was raised very easily from Black people who believed in either the producer or the writers. The investors represented the average theatre-goer. Hard worker. Average of $10,000 income or above. Average people. Now one might assume that the writers and the people who believe in writers are indeed one and the same. Not so! There is a system between them. There might be a theatre owner different from the usual slum landlord. There also might be a union that came into existence before Black people were figured into the overall scheme of things. There most certainly is that audience which I mentioned earlier. And finally, there is the media, such as *The New York Times, New York Post, Daily News, Newsweek, New Yorker, Nation,* etc. Their critics are all white. They don't care what you are talking about if you are not talking to them. *A Black Quartet* wasn't talking to them. It *had* to make it by reaching Black people. If it couldn't, then it would have to close. It found Black people for only six months.

If we can say that the present form that "theatre" is struggling against is real, then *A Black Quartet* is revolutionary Black art by virtue of its writers, its staff, its performers, and the content of the plays themselves. It could be called Black theatre if there is such a thing. But (and this is a dangerous point, but I'm going to be dangerous!) if Black people can't do for it what they can do for James Brown, Aretha Franklin, the Baptist Church, the Muslims, the NAACP and Smokey Robinson, then one should question which forms really represent Black theatre.

Will Black theatre in America please stand and take a bow?

Busting Out of Bags

BLACK THEATRE HAS COME TO mean the same things to Black people that Black revolution means to Black people. Black people are willing to die for what they believe to be right for the greater good. We are willing to die for what we believe rightfully belongs to us. We must assume that if white people or any people get in the way, they must (and will) be destroyed. The Euro-American theatre as it exists now is in the path of Black theatre. It must be destroyed. Black writers no longer try to write for the Americn theatre as they tried to do during pre-revolution days. Black writers are writing to and for Black people. And Black people are now listening. This is because they know they are being talked to and not talked at. The Black playwright's goal is to teach and enlighten through the use of the stage. To the Black playwright, American theatre is irrelevant.

Black playwrights moved one step behind black jazz musicians when their work took on the new forms of communication. Notice it in LeRoi Jones' *Slaveship* and Gylan Kain's *Epitaph for the Coagulated Trinity*. Sounds are as important as the visuals. Actors' voices become musical instruments. Jones takes the actors one step farther when he creates gaps for improvisation. The gaps can only be filled if the performer understands the Black life-style.

All the plays herein are busting out of traditional theatre bags. As you read them, you will also find that the playwrights are demanding change by any means necessary. Beyond these plays the writers are also pacemakers in the development of Black theatre in this country, busting it out of bags.

Gilbert Moses developed his awareness of the life-style during five years as artistic director of the Free Southern Theater. For those of you who may not know about it, the Free Southern Theater tours the cotton fields and backwoods of Lousiana, Texas, Mississippi, Georgia, and Alabama. The people of these states are the same people who migrate to the North looking for the promised land. Moses' work is always directed to them. He must understand them. Slightly the blues. You will find the same quality in Gil Moses' play *Roots*.

LeRoi Jones' style, on the other hand, comes from different forms of jazz. He was a jazz critic in Greenwich Village in the late fifties when most Black musicians worked there. This was before he wrote plays. It was not, however, before he wrote poetry. Jones' plays can best be described as Black poetic jazz. The thrust and importance of this revolutionary form became evident in 1964 when LeRoi Jones opened the Black Arts Revolutionary Theatre in Harlem. The white establishment, which had not cared at all about Harlem and the little-theatre movement, countered by cutting off all funds for the theatre. But if an artist is to bust bags, a lack of money should not be able to stop him. The following year LeRoi Jones moved back to Newark and formed the Spirit House Movers, a group of talented actors, writers, and poets. At present they are the best example of what Black theatre is all about. Their plays range the gamut of the Black life-style. LeRoi Jones writes and directs. They have toured the country several times. Their work is highly imitated by college students and so-called radical theatre groups that strive to be daring. Spirit House Movers are the pace-setters in the Black theatre movement.

Ed Bullins wrote in San Francisco across the bay from Oakland. He is one of the founders of Black House. He worked directly with most of the brothers and sisters who founded the Black Panther Party for Self-Defense. Cultural Nationalist and Revolutionaries used the same headquarters for all their activities. I only point this out so that Bullins' work can be clearly understood. The violent turning points in most of Bullins' work comes from a writer who has witnessed the changes that Black people have been going through. The most violent confrontations have resulted in the better immediate changes. The destruction of the madame and everything that she represents in Bullins' *The Gentlemen Caller* is an ideal example of what I am talking about.

All the writers in this collection are founders of their own theatre companies. It was probably the only way that they could get the message to Black people. Until 1965, Black literature very seldom received attention from major publications. The new awareness and the ascendency of Black pride demand that the white world recognize Black people will not accept the typical white writer's interpretation of blackness.

There are about seventy Black theatres in this country. We are not counting the countless theatres in universities and colleges. All the plays in this collection have been performed to a Black audience. Ben Caldwell is produced on an average of three times per week. If the Black groups could afford to pay the writers, all of them would earn about eight thousand dollars per year. Jones, Bullins, Caldwell, Milner and Garrett would probably earn a great deal more. I want to emphasize this point: if you are not familiar with the writer, do not assume he is unknown.

As I said earlier, to be familiar with the Euro-American theatre doesn't mean one is familiar with Black theatre. The Black theatres do not as a rule produce white plays; white theatres as a rule will do one Black play per year but only if it has a Black and white cast.

In terms of so-called professional productions, only three of the plays received New York productions. I produced Bullins' *The Gentlemen Caller* Off-Broadway in July of 1969 as part of *A Black Quartet*. I co-produced LeRoi Jones' *Slaveship* with Chelsea Theatre Center in the Bedford-Stuyvesant section of Brooklyn. It later moved Off-Broadway for a limited run in New York and then on to Europe. Joe White's *Old Judge Moses is Dead* was produced by the Urban Arts Corps and directed by Vinnette Carroll. What happened when these plays opened to Euro-American-oriented audiences, ranged the gamut from appreciation to open attempts to stop the shows. Even before *A Black Quartet* opened, some theatre owners let it be known that they did not want a Bullins or a Jones play in their theatre. However, the white critics hailed the plays. The theatre where *Slaveship* played mysteriously caught fire and the fire department declared it unsafe for a theatrical production. Three weeks later the department declared it safe for a white production.

Black playwrights tend to refuse white theatres when their plays are requested because, often, their plays are given bad productions by white-oriented producers. These producers usually direct the plays to the white audience, playing on white fears and superstitions. Black playwrights are not trying to prove anything to white people anymore. They stopped wasting their time and energy trying to prove to white people that they knew how to write plays.

It has been stated that a play on the written page is less than seventy percent of the total vision of that play. The audience makes the play live or die. When a play and its audience understand each other, they become one. When they do not understand each other, the play either loses its value or remains at its seventy percent. Know while you are reading these plays that to see them would be of a much more lasting value. Only two actors who understand the Black life-style can make one really know what the mother and her son, Johnny, must have endured in the scene from Garrett's *And We Own The Night*. Ditto, Evan Walker's *The Message,* when the two brothers confront each other. Many whites are aware that Black theatre of this magnitude is directed to Black people. They stay away from it. They want to be lied to; they don't want Black theatre to talk to and try to teach Blacks. That would mean Blacks are showing who their enemies are.

To understand conditions at any given point in our history, one only has to study the literature of the period. The plays in this collection give a clear understanding of the pride and new awareness of Black people. Some of the plays are extremely funny—for example, Paul Carter Harrison's *Pavane For A Dead-Pan Minstrel* and Ronald Milner's *The Monster*. Evan Walker's *The Message* is perhaps the most angry play ever written. I think it's because Walker had so much hope and love for this country. Jimmy Garrett's *And We Own The Night* is the most frightening and without a doubt the Blackest play that I have read.

The conditions that produced the playwrights are evident everywhere; from the government right down to any dark street in an unknown neighborhood. Most Black literature of this period is about the *destruction of America. Heroes are Crazy Horse, Denmark Vesey and Patrice Lumumba.*

What the Black playwright needs since he doesn't have Broadway, Off-Broadway, the regional theatres, and the university theatres is a continual training ground. This training ground must be similar to if not actually the seventy theatres that are already located in the Black communities across the U.S.A. Our critics will be the people in those communities. Black disc jockeys will be to the Black theatres that the *New York Times* is to Euro-American theatre.

It's unfortunate that no playwright in this collection can survive on the income from the plays he writes. Ed Bullins, who is the playwright in residence at New Lafayette Theatre in Harlem, is the only writer in the collection with a job that can be considered as playwright. However, he must do much more there. He edits *Black Theatre Magazine* and directs Black Theatre Workshop. Some Black playwrights are offered jobs as screenwriters by some of the Hollywood studios. Most of the jobs are rejected by the writers because they cannot get control of the final product—but these offers are few and far between.

The theatres in the Black communities, then, can be the breeding and proving ground for new Black playwrights, if they will but see the opportunity and accept the responsibility.

One should also note that the publication of Black plays and Black literature will automatically get the plays and the literature to the public. An upsurge in publication also means an upsurge in Black theatre. Some Black plays that were given bad productions in New York are given excellent productions in other cities. The white press is meaningless in the Black communities. A bad review in a paper that they do not read is meaningless.

The Failure
of Educational Theatre

EDUCATIONAL THEATRE AND
the Black community have been at odds since my beginning in theatre. I don't
see a coming-together of these two institutions until they begin to understand
each other. It is the duty of an educational institution to serve the community
that supports it. With educational theatre, that is not happening. I would like
to go back to 1959-60 and establish a context for what I wish to say. To talk
about directing Black plays, I must constantly remind you of exactly where I
am coming from.

In 1959-60, I was a student at Wayne University. It had not become a
state university at that time and it did not have a theatre department although it
did have a theatre. Drama was presented through the speech department. I was
in the speech department and I appeared in two plays in the two years that I
was there. One play was Eugene O'Neill's *Emperor Jones,* the other Marc
Connelly's *Green Pastures.* Among my predecessors at the university were
Lloyd Richards and Walter Mason. Mr. Richards appeared in two plays in four
years; Mr. Mason appeared in four plays in four years. I think Mr. Mason had
more exposure because he had a strong bass voice and could sing. This
university and the Black community had absolutely nothing in common.

I don't remember too much about *Emperor Jones* except that I fired two
shots at the third apparition. The gun was empty when I tried to shoot the sixth
one. *Green Pastures* is a little clearer. Aaron's walking stick would not turn
into a snake and the director was drunk most of the time. He felt that he should
have been in New York theatre and that Detroit was too small for his talents.

I suppose it is obvious that *Emperor Jones* and *Green Pastures* are not
two of my favorite plays. I had been seeing them for years at schools in the
Detroit area; every issue of *Theater Arts* had ads indicating that universities
were performing the plays as part of their season. Both Walter Mason and
Lloyd Richards had appeared in the plays while at the University.

No new writer could get produced on the university scene in the late fifties. There's no point in even discussing whether a Black writer made it to the university. It seemed to me, at the time, that if I wanted to make a career in the theatre arts, it was futile to continue at a place where I would be confined to these two plays by white Americans. Of course, the white students were appearing in five or six productions per semester.

These facts made me aware that educational theatre in the university was not at all concerned about its Black students. Educational theatre was a game, and the game wasn't even real. If one could discuss Tennessee Williams, Arthur Miller, Henrik Ibsen, O'Neill, and William Shakespeare he could get through without problems.

I find, in retrospect, that the professional theatre schools I later attended prepared me for a better understanding of theatre. And I came to understand that the public library is the only real educational theatre for a Black person working the theatre.

With that out of the way, we now can deal with directing the Black play. Directors of Black plays in the professional theatre are so hampered by their authors and producers that only a very few of their ideas are realized. The more influential playwrights like Ed Bullins, Amiri Baraka, Lonnie Elder and Charles Gordone select their own directors. New writers may insist on the director but they don't often get their choice. Because of the hit-or-miss system in New York, a writer has only one chance. But that is also the case with the director and the producer. Since the director is the weakest link in the chain of these three, he catches the most hell.

Yet there is another problem. I think it is caused by there being so few opportunities in New York theatre. A director will read a play; he will know in front that he hates it, that it should be completely rewritten. Yet he will tell the author, the producer, the leading lady, et al., that it is the greatest play he has ever read. Then, after his contract has been signed, he wants the entire play rewritten. The author, of course, isn't going to do this; the producer has only four weeks in time and money, so he must look for another director. Meanwhile, the theatre has been rented, the actors hired. In other words, the producer has entered the taxi and the meter will continue clicking away until he gets out. Getting out for the producer is the opening night of the play.

Unfortunately, at this particular time, there are only about ten Black directors, and over half of these don't see themselves as *Black* directors. I often question their reason for their "racelessness" since they never get an offer to direct any plays other than Black plays. As a matter of record, all their little fame came as a result of directing Black plays. Very few Black directors are invited to direct at educational institutions. And I know at the base of this is a fear that they may direct something too militant or something violently Black. But the fact is that they also want to direct Shakespeare, Ibsen and Miller to prove something to those who control access to the theatre.

On campuses around the country one finds young Blacks either from Black student unions or off-shoots of the theatre departments directing their own thing in small improvised theatres. And the theatres are often packed. They don't have sets or lights or know anything about stage direction, but they know their audience. As they continue to direct and produce and build audiences, the existing theatres on the campuses are going to be taken over or destroyed.

I would like to think that when I select a play to produce that the play will attract the same audience of Blacks and young whites. On the university scene, they are the ones who are tired of the traditional. One's level of consciousness cannot be raised by the traditional theatre. And I feel that it is my duty as a producer of Black plays and Black art to do this—raise the level of consciousness in Black people. Plays I do are generally about Black people struggling to overcome some personal or family problem. I am aware that white plays have been produced dealing with some of the same problems. I am aware that plays will be compared. That is the nature of the theatre. But I am gratified to find that the audience that I hope to attract usually hasn't seen that other play. For example, Baraka's *Slaveship* for $2 per ticket is different from Grotowski's *Acropolis* for $10 per ticket—even though the *Drama Review,* an educational quarterly, may think they are the same. I know who saw what.

The Black plays I am drawn to are often about 60 percent of the total vision. Because so few Black writers have had the opportunity to be around theatre a great deal, they lack knowledge of some of the mechanics of putting a play on paper. I expect a director to supply about 25 percent of the vision; the actors and production another 15 percent. All this may sound mechanical, but it has a great deal to do with directors' attitudes on Black plays. Many white directors reject Black plays because their understanding of the Black life-style isn't comprehensive enough to supply the necessary artistic imput. However, there are some well-crafted plays by Black writers which would be more suitable for university theatre than for professional theatre. I've found that most plays that are well-crafted are written by teachers and professors who have studied craft for so long they've forgotten their subject matter.

I am not interested in producing plays about Black-white conflict. Plays I do are usually all-Black. A writer told me once that all-Black plays were very difficult to get produced at universities even though they were listed in Samuel French's catalogue. He was told by several universities that they needed plays for Black and white students.

In the beginning I implied that university and Black theatre seemed to be getting together, that the relationship seemed a little better. I've had two very good opportunities at observing this improvement: one as a professional actor-director and the other as a producer-director on *A Black Quartet,* four one-act plays by Baraka, Bullins, Ben Caldwell, and Ronald Milner. A few years ago we took the American Place Theatre production of Ron Milner's *Who's Got His Own* on tour to New York state universities. We found that while most of the students who saw the play were white, they asked meaningful questions about the Black life-style—questions that I feel must be answered not for them but for ourselves. Those white boys will be graduating soon, taking over from their fathers, assuming responsibilities—what I am saying is that they are going to be running this country if we don't watch out. And most of them don't want the responsibility. During the open discussions with the Black cast, some of the white boys said it was the first time they had talked to Black people for more than ten minutes.

On the other occasion, during the tour of *A Black Quartet,* white theatre departments found the plays too "irrevelant." However, the Black student unions found the plays very important and booked them into the universities. In the two occasions, I found that, in educational theatre, what might be important to white students may not be of interest to Black students, and vice versa. However, most of the plays that I do are educational. I am concerned about raising the level of consciousness in Black people and the audience.

Directing the Black play must include an understanding of the community that the play is written for. I have seen so many plays destroyed by directors whose heads were someplace other than the Black community. I must confess that I've produced several plays that were flops. But they failed for two reasons that I was able to catch at an early stage. They were aimed at a student and Black audience, and both ticket price and time of production were wrong. They also were hampered by personnel whose chief ambition is to "make it" in the white theatrical world. So you might say the failures were educational for me and my associates.

Again, as I have implied throughout, there are some signs that things are getting a little better. Electronic video recorders (EVR) and cable television (CATV) will be in almost every school in a few years. EVR cassettes will have all the so-called classics, as well as lectures by the most respected artists in theatre. All one will need is a CATV installation. The classics will be captured on video as they are in books. Educational institutions must then look for the new, the innovative. I think the new and the innovative are in Black theatre.

Sacred Songs: Rhythm and Blues and Yesterday

You're a thousand miles away
But I still have your love to
Remember you by. [1]

Been so long since I held you tight
Been so long since I kissed you
goodnight.

Remember the good old days!
Moonglows, Flamingoes, Orioles!
Clovers, Drifters, Spaniels,
Coasters, Dells, Harptones, etc. [2]

WHY HAVE WE NOSTALGICALLY gravitated towards groups in our search for Blackness? Rhythm and blues? Even gangs, and families? We have always felt saddened by their disappearance, by their death, by their downfall. We remember when so-and-so used to sing with the _____, when someone else was killed by the _____ gang, and when the _____ family moved out of town. Is it because they are all a part of us?

With rhythm and blues groups, the companies or labels like Roulette, Atlantic, Mercury, Chess, Gee, Dootone, Vee Jay, King, Chance, Bluebird, Okeh, Specialty, Natural, Jubilee, End, Herald-Ember, Federal, Rama, and so many smaller labels which were really subsidiaries of the larger labels, did not treat the progression as a graduation for a new Black music. Right off, you know that we all know who was responsible for the exploitation; you know that they thought they knew more about our Blackness than we did. And that they were the ones who would manage, produce, and sign us to contracts that not even they could understand. And they would pay us one cent royalty and we seldom got that. Ertegun, Feld, Ram, Shiffman, Wexler, Leiber, Stoller, Dowd, Levy, Treadwell, Backarach, Asch, Lomax, Freed, etc.

And we let them do it! If this is not true, all the groups were happy. They all got a fair count. None was insane, alcoholics, or junkies. Little Willie John, Frankie Lyman, Hudie Ledbetter, James Sheppard and Clyde McPhatter, one of the founders of the R & B movement, did not die broke and heartbroken. These people who came to control our music also exploited our street gangs and destroyed our families. And it is all because we let them. We let them because we did not understand why we were together in the first place or the value of what we created.

In the early fifties our rhythm was a studied mannerism. We lived by it. Some called it names like cool, hip, fine, pimp, game, etc. Our dress helped to define it. Shoes, pants, shirt, and hat. Our friends also defined us by their association with us. We were all peacocks; our rhythm and our lives existed in direct relation to our sexual prowess. If we had made a baby the time we were fifteen or sixteen, we were given the title of *men* or *women*. It was important that our progression from boys and girls be ahead of us.

Our blues at the time was our need to ignore the reality of our situation. The situation was as unreal as our existing reality. Blues which Ralph Ellison has described as suppressed intellectual energy expressed physically. What we had learned in the early fifties was to express all those problems we had at that early age, all those problems we knew existed with our mothers and fathers, our sisters and cousins, our aunts and uncles; what we had learned was to hide it from that other world in another life-style. The ability to hide it was our rhythm. The knowledge of it was our blues.

Our rhythm and our blues. Rhythm and Blues. That's what our groups were called in the fifties. If we look back to the forties and on back to the thirties, we know Ma Rainey, Bessie Smith, Hudie Ledbetter, and Blind Lemon were progressions to the present. To move out of that, out of a definition of it, we moved into the sixties, into the rock and roll of it, and on into the soul of it. But now, looking back to my formative years of the early fifties, most events remembered are Rhythm-and-Blues benchmarks. This is a memory; a benchmark, if you will. I will try and recall Gwen Lewis of that period. When I think of the music of the period, I think of her. She was my starting point then.

She lived in this America. The Detroit of the automobile. Her family was not all together. A father was missing. She had cousins or uncles and most of their lives were affected by the steel mills and the automobile plants in that city. She lived on the northend. There were other ends like the southend, westend, eastend. These ends only meant that Black people, at that time, moved no further in that direction. In this northend, Gwen lived on Chandler and Oakland. She loved R & B music. She especially loved Bill Ward and the Dominoes.

Later I would return to the area. It would be after high school, nearing 1957. I would carry with me a melancholy mood; a forced loneliness. I would be searching for little signs that would indicate that I had not existed and would not exist in vain. This mood of the time was so evident among most of us. We were at the end of one movement and at the beginning of another. We who had finished high school at such great odds were now trying to find some indication that the next step was in us. How do I remember the end of 1956? No, not by graduating high school, but by a record by the Heartbeats, *A Thousand Miles Away* as sung by James (Shep) Sheppard. It was one of the big hits of 1956. Its emotional and religious impact touched me directly because I wanted all my women friends to be reincarnations of Gwen Lewis. I wanted to suffer her loss.

Your're a thousand miles away
But I still have your love to remember you by
Oh my darling dry your eyes
Daddy's coming home soon.

On my knees every day
All I do is pray
Baby just for you
Hope you always want me to

Daddy's coming home soon

It may be on a Sunday morning
It may be on a Tuesday afternoon
But no matter what the day is
I'm going to make it my business
To get home soon. [3]

We all suffered Shep's loss in the dawning seventies, after the Black revolution of the sixties. Shep was killed by gangsters.

Item: *Variety* magazine, August 2, 1972: N.Y. Police exec ties roulette records with Mafia: Levy denies it.

Allegations that Roulette Records is linked to organized crime have been made by William McCarthy, deputy N.Y. police commissioner. McCarthy, speaking on the Victor Reisel show on WEVD, N.Y., Monday night (7/31/72) said that Tommy (Ryan) Eboli, a reputed Mafia figure who was killed in gangland style in Brooklyn a couple of weeks ago, was general manager for sales and promotion for Promo Records, a distributor in Paterson, N.J.

McCarthy said that Promo Records was interlocked with Roulette Records since both companies had the same president, Morris Levy, whom he did not name. McCarthy said that Eboli's salary was $1,000 per week.

In the early fifties, the South was not far behind. It had been the South of Jackson, Mobile, Baldwin Springs, and Bessemer, Alabama. I tell you this now because I want you to understand our common ground. It was not far behind for any of us. Mine was 1949. At that time I was eleven years old. And at that time in Detroit, there would be movies at the Grant Theater on Russell Street. There would be R & B shows at the Echo Theater on Oakland. There would be Barthwell's Ice Cream, and there would also be discoveries of unheard of areas of the northend which only us eleven-year-olds knew existed. To us, as I look back, it must have been something like Columbus discovering America.

The family (our group) consisted of my mother and me, my aunt and her two children, cousin Errol and cousin Gwen. We lived at Oakland and Euclid in a very small three-room aparatment. Our family worked for white people. All our neighbors worked for white people. The pimps and the hustlers and the singers did not work for white people, we thought. So, in all honesty, we children had two roads cut for us. We would be like our parents or we would be like the pimps, the hustlers, or the R & B singers.

A man would come by about once a month. He had been a friend of my aunt's husband. They went hunting together in years past for possums and coons. He was very sad but his laughter would affect us all. He carried a lot of photographs from World War II. He would show them to us and we would ask questions. There were many dead bodies in the photographs. Sometimes the man would cry and tell us through tear-filled eyes to stick together. My mother always offered him a drink and he always refused. My aunt would ask him to eat; he would. After he ate he would leave. I wanted to tell you about *Golden Teardrops* by the Flamingoes but when I hear the lyrics I think of the man with the photographs and his tears.

Golden teardrop
I remember when/ you
Fell/ from the eyes of my love
You made me reconsider
What a fool I've been
And swear to God/ I'll say no more
By all the stars above
Golden teardrops
You haunt my memories.
The reason you came/ was because
Of me/ you made me see that cloud
Over the stars/ so go back/ where
You came from/ she won't need you
*   anymore*
I never realized that I was unfair
To a love that was really sincere
I never knew how much you really cared.
So darling put away your tears, cause
I'll remember/ no matter where you be
In a crowded room/ or busy street
Or a cottage by the sea/ darling
We'll be in the heights/ throughout
Eternity/ I'll remember
Those golden teardrops for me.[4]
(Repeat)

The Grady family lived across the hall. Mr. and Mrs. Grady, the daughter, and James Grady. James was thirteen. He had a paper route. He delivered the *Pittsburgh Courier* and the *Michigan Chronicle*. He had money. He would take us to the Echo Theatre to see the R & B shows. He could sing bass. He could sing *Sixty Minute Man* just like the Dominoes. He knew little Willie John and Sugar Chile Robinson who lived near us. James' sister was older. She had large piles of records. She would play *Crying in the Chapel* for hours. Then she would play *Baby, Please Don't Go*. She had an old gramophone and she would wind it very slowly so that the music would *sound good*.

Baby, please don't go
Baby, please don't go
Back to New Orleans
You know I love you so . . .[5]

But *Crying in the Chapel* was her favorite. She said listening to it was like being in church.

You saw me crying in the chapel
The tears I shed were tears of joy
I know the meaning of contentment
I am happy with the Lord.

Just a plain and simple chapel
Where all the people go to pray
I pray the Lord that I'll grow stronger
As I live from day to day.

You'll search and you'll search
But you'll never find
Nowhere on earth to find peace of mind.

Take your troubles to the chapel
Get down on your knees and pray
Then your burden will be lighter
And you'll surely find a way. [6]

The records had cost her forty-nine cents each. She didn't mind spending that much money because she was in love with Sonny Till. She had all the Orioles records: *It's Too Soon To Know, Baby, Please Don't Go, Forgive and Forget*. She would let us sit and listen if we were very quiet.

Gwen Lewis was my girlfriend. She was my girl simply because that was the way I wanted it. We never talked about it; we talked about other things. My friend James taught me how to kiss Gwen. He would demonstrate by kissing her, telling me to watch. Our group was James Grady, my cousins, and a boy named James Mathews.

Gwen Lewis and I would walk home from Breitmeyer School. She was upset on this last walk because Clyde McPhatter had said he was going to leave Billy Ward and the Dominoes. Her two favorite songs were *The Bells* and *Have Mercy, Mercy, Baby*. She would sing *The Bells* like Clyde.

There were four black horses
With eyes of flaming red
There's roses tied with ribbon
All around my baby's head

The bells are ringing . . . [7]

I would tell her that I was scared of songs about death. We would sit on her porch and we would hold hands. She would always sing to me like in the movies. She would deliberately imitate some white singer singing to a guy in a film. We would end up laughing.

One day, not long after that walk, she moved away. I went to her house. It was empty. No one knew where the family moved. James tried to help me find her. But she left no signs. She was not part of any group. She was alone.

Have mercy, mercy, mercy, baby
I know I done you wrong
Now my heart is full of sorrow
You take me back where I belong.

I've been a good for nothing
I lied and cheated too
Well, I'm reaping oh my darling
And I don't know what to do.

So, have mercy, mercy, mercy, baby
Please don't slam that door
'Cause I know if you refuse me
I'd never be the same no more. [8]

Now try and understand the loss of a first love. It was the end of a created fantasy world of tomorrow. Our ghetto contained us. We dreamed beyond it. Most of us selected a secret someone to transcend the place with. I selected Gwen Lewis—selected her too soon and without her knowledge or my knowledge of it. Do you understand what your first loss was like? By definition of things past and forever lost to one who never had anything to lose, a relationship is golden, a companion is forever. If the loss is a first loss, it will move you to a group that you can merge into. It did that for me. If you wore Mr. B. (Billy Eckstine) shirts, Stetson shoes, Dobbs or Knox Twenties, Hi-Lo Shirts from Hot Sams, gang-warred with the Shakers, danced at the Madison, roller-skated at the Arcadia, you probably know what I mean. A group was necessary; a group was golden. I want to believe that the R & B groups came together through the same understanding. Why else would I listen to them and enjoy them so?

School was a discovery. At eleven years and straight from Alabama, I entered the Detroit school system. The system welcomed me by putting me back to the first grade. It was not uncommon to put Black children from the

South two or three grades behind. The Southern school system was supposed to be so terrible. I was at the mercy of the Detroit system as most Black children are. Most of our fathers and mothers could not speak for us. My mother could not talk to white people. It is part of what we've come to understand as the perpetual lie. The white person is lying, the Black listener knows it. The white liar knows the Black listener knows he is lying. The white liar becomes vicious for being caught lying. To counter that, the Black listener refuses to refute the white liar or even to look him in the face.

So, at eleven years, I was in the first grade. I know now it was because I spoke *Black English* and had learned to exist in another rhythm. But the next five years, I attended summer school and I came out ahead of the system. It was due to the help of one teacher, a Mr. Finger. He was an art teacher at Breitmeyer. I loved art. I loved to draw Cisco Kid, John Garfield, and black horses. Mr. Finger would teach me in his spare time; always taking the class to places like the Art Institute and encouraging us when we formed singing groups. He would often say, "Young man"—I wonder if he ever knew my name—"Young man, we have to stick together as a Black group, as a Black family."

Julius Williams was the terror of the school. He was sixteen. He enjoyed fighting teachers and singing in class. He had a singing group and a gang. When the teacher left the room he would always sing, *One Mint Julep,* by the Clovers:

One early morning
As I went walking
I met a woman/ started talking
I took her home/ to get a few drinks
But all I had was a mint julep.

One mint julep was the cause of it all

I don't remember just/ how it started
But all I know is/ we shoulda parted
I stole a kiss and then another . . . [9]

One of his best friends was a member of the *Five Jets*. They became very popular for a tune called *I Got It*. It was rumored that after Julius graduated from Moore Intermediate School for Boys he joined the Shaker Gang. It was also rumored that he made a record with the Royal Jokers.

In the years 1952 to 1955 we listened to the onslaught of R & B music.

We didn't call it that until some years later. But we did try to sing it and some of us were successful. Many groups were split by the Korean War. Members of singing groups and gangs were drafted or joined. Families were heartbroken when relatives were killed. As boys came home, others joined or got drafted. They all said they were going to kill some Koreans. Very few felt they would be killed.

Item: January, 1952, Detroit's Negro population was 300,000.

We moved to the east side. I had to leave behind my group. All the gains I felt I had made at that young age had to be left behind. I thought that the world would end for me. I would never find Gwen Lewis. Why did we have to move, I thought, right at the time I was so popular; right at the time all the students and teachers knew that I really existed? And most importantly, right at the time I was appointed captain of the safety patrol? Surely, I thought, there would be no streetcars as far as the east side. No Grant or Echo Theatres.

We live on Heidelberg Street between Elmwood and Ellery. We had the downstairs flat. Upstairs lived the Brown family. Mr. and Mrs. Brown, their son Lincoln, and their daughter, Juanita. Juanita would be murdered a few years later in Brooklyn and her killer would not be found. Next door, on our right, lived the McNeal family. The family consisted of four brothers and three sisters. Ernest McNeal became one of my best friends. On our left, I remember a Mr. and Mrs. Cooper. I remember he was a master at poker, Tonk and blackjack. My uncle and Mr. Cooper were partners. They would travel miles to find a card game. I mention the people as I knew them—part of a family.

At Smith School, next to Franklin Settlement, I met Leonard Brown, Willie Jackson, and John French. We were members of the Settlement, and after the Settlement closed at ten o'clock, we hung out at Herndon's Candy store on Elmwood. Our days and our evenings were discoveries of the games, the girls, and the music there. The northend was far behind. And as Langston Hughes has told us, when one is on a borderline, the distance between here and there is nowhere. We all could sing. We sang in the lounge of the settlement and we sang on the corner in front of Herndon's candy store. Ernest and John could sing better. Ernest was a tenor; he could sing *Blue Moon*. John was a bass; he, like James Grady, could sing *Sixty Minute Man*. I was a Clovers fan. I would sing lead on *Yes, It's You*. We would make our piano with our voices and go into it:

Whaaaa aaahhh
Makes my love come tumblin' dooownnn
Makes a lover from a cloownn
Yes, it's you
Yes, it's you

You drive away my aches and pains
calls my name so sweet and plain
Yes, it's you
Yes, it's you

You stole my heart
The minute your lips met mine . . . [10]

Most of the groups that rehearsed at the settlement had been together for a long time. The relationship went beyond the mere singing. The Diablos used to rehearse *The Wind* there long before it was recorded. It is one of the most beautiful R & B songs ever recorded. And Nolan Strong's high lead voice is the most beautifully controlled tenor in R & B music.

Wind/ wind
Bloo-ooh wind
Wind/ wind
Bloo-ooh wind

When the cool summer breeze
Sends a chill down my spine
And I long for my love's sweet caress
I know she has gone
But my love lingers on
In a dream that the wind brings to me

I remember her sweet kiss
In the cool summer breeze
As she lay warm and tender in my arms

And here Nolan would rap to the girl, telling her how beautiful it *had* been. Then, he would sing to us again:

I know she has gone
But my love lingers on
In a dream that the wind brings to me. [11]

Marvin Black who lived down the street from me at Heidelberg and Elmwood rehearsed at the settlement with his group. He changed his name to Marv Johnson when he left his group. Marv was one of the best. In 1959 when Motown exploded onto the scene, he was one of the first artists to be signed. Another group was the Detroit Emeralds who sang at some of the dances. Mitchell, one of the members, ran a restaurant on Vernor Highway owned by his parents. We would dance in the backyard of the restaurant. Even though most of the group lived on the northend, they had an east side sound (yes, groups sound different from different sections of a city). They were guided by Chico Hamilton. One of Chico's younger brothers was in the Emeralds.

Later, in my high school years at Cass Tech, Chico Hamilton would become very famous as a basketball player. But in 1954, he quit suddenly and disappeared. The white and Black press bemoaned his departure in the sports section. You see, he had been named high school All-American in his first year on the team. In the late fifties and early sixties he re-emerged as Ronnie Savoy—a very talented R & B record producer and songwriter. He owned a recording company in Newark, New Jersey. He produced hit records for the Drifters and the Fantastic Four. And he was one of the first brothers to write music for television commercials. I met him again in the beginning of the seventies and the years between 1954 and 1971 seemed indistinguishable. Poet Norman Jordan has told us, *In the last days/ all things return to what they were.*

Our after-school activities were basketball and music. Miller High School was in the area and most of the team basketball players were members of the settlement. They were the best. Their photographs in action appeared in the *Michigan Chronicle* every week. They also had the best coach, Will Robinson. And he was Black and he didn't take no shit. Every kid on the east side wanted to go to Miller High School after intermediate school. The five of us vowed we would go to Miller. We did everything together; we were such good friends.

At the time, our world seemed destined to last forever. Ernest was the best fighter. John French was also feared everywhere because the French family's reputation went with him, with us. On this east side, house parties on Friday and Saturday evenings were our glory. Ernest and John could dance. Leonard, Willie and I were the pretty boys. We pranced in our Hi-Lo shirts, expensive Stetsons and Stacy Adams shoes, Knox and Dobbs hats. We were not yet fifteen years old but we were living adult lives. As Langston Hughes has told us, *In the quarters of the Negroes/ a nickel cost a dime/ living twenty years in ten . . .* Our dream was to own a Cadillac and to pimp like Ted and Adolph.

In our house parties we searched for dark corners for our slow grinding. Our music at these parties were the Chantels' *Maybe*, the Flamingoes' *I Only Have Eyes for You* and *Golden Teardrops*, the Spaniels' *Goodnight Sweetheart Goodnight*, the Harptones' *Sunday Kind of Love*, the Turbans' *When You Dance*, the Clovers' *Blue Velvet*, the Crows' *Gee*, the Moonglows' *Most of All* and *We Go Together*, and the Penguins' *Earth Angel*. Our house parties and our music could not exist without each other. The house parties were in basements and the lights would always be down low. We would dance our slow grind or we would dance our slow bop. It was always slow and cool. We had not yet been contaminated by *American Bandstand*. House-party streets were Kirby, Hastings, Burns, Benson, Elba, Mt. Elliot, Canton, Meldrum, etc. One's reputation must supersede him; girls must be expecting him. One must expect revenges to be met from another house-party incident. Our girls went by names like Candy, Kay Williams, Leona, Margie Craighead, Tuttie, Carol Hinton, Lodie, Fruittie, Liz, Beverly, Tootsie, Willie Mae, Johnnie Mae, Marie Lewis, Dumpty, etc.

At our house parties we loved to hear Hank Ballard and the Midnighters sing *Work with me Annie/ Better git it while the gittin is good/ So good/ so good....* [12] The Midnighters told us about ourselves. Things that we all understood because of the simplicity of it. We loved the Five Royales singing: *Crazy, Crazy, Crazy; I got a girl named Millie/ Millie, she act so silly/ Millie's got a sister names Tillie/ Now, ain't that Crazy/ crazy, crazy/ Ain't that crazy/ I'm talkin' outta my head!* [13] Looking back, as we often do, before the Midnighters changed their name in 1954, they were known as the Royales. Don't you remember *Moonrise, The Shrine of St. Cecelia,* and *Every Beat of My Heart? —With every beat of my heart/ There's a beat for you/ And everything I do/ I do for you....* [14] So we would laugh and push each other and our girls would laugh with us. Other times we were so cool, we never said a word for the duration of a party. The mood set by the record would direct our actions.

The singers had a total image. We did not define them by any one single song. We had seen them at the Warfield Theatre, the Madison Ballroom, and the Echo Theatre. In the basements, when we danced to *Crazy, Crazy, Crazy* and *Think,* we also danced to *Baby Don't Do It* and *Help Me Somebody*. Our singing groups had a total image, be they the Clovers, the Drifters, the Spaniels, the Coasters, or the Penguins.

When we added rhythm to our blues, we did it so that our existence would be less of a burden than could be detected by the casual observer. The observer could see no hope, no understanding of our confusion. But we all felt it within us, even the observer if he was Black. It could not be hidden by marcelled heads, diamonds, Cadillacs, clothes, or white girls. And our blues singers kept telling us in no uncertain terms that we were blue. We could not lie and pretend otherwise. What Bessie Smith, Billie Holiday, T. Bone Walker, John Lee Hooker, Dinah Washington, and Johnny Ace told us, we had to deal with internally. But we did not have to deal with those things — those blues externally if we could create an alternate. The rhythm became an alternate.

The group and the rhythm became easily identifiable. Their *sound* and their *rhythm* became easily identifiable. Their *sound* and their *rhythm* became their trademark. I cannot show you the background of the R & B groups, the choreographed steps, the *doo-wah-wo-oooh sa ra,* the harmony. It cannot be defined. Philadelphia had its sound and rhythm as did Chicago, New York, New Jersey, Indiana, and Detroit. In trying, I'll just say, movements were choreographed and comedy routines perfected, for every song. The Royal Jokers, for example, were known for throwing an imaginary bee on each other, then dancing and gyrating until it was found. The Spaniels were known for Pookie Hudson's lead and Gerald Gregory's beautiful bass. They were at their best in the million-seller *Goodnight Sweetheart Goodnight:*

Goodnight Sweetheart well it's time to go
(Repeat)
I hate to leave you
But I really must say
Oh, goodnight sweetheart, goodnight

Well, it's three o'clock in the morning
Baby, I just can't git right
Well, I hate to leave you baby
Don't mean maybe
Because I love you so

And here Gregory would come in with that beautiful bass:

Dat-dah-da-da-dah

Pookie would come back with:

Mother, oh and your father wouldn't
Like it if I stayed here too long
One kiss and I'll be going
You know I hate to . . . [15]

The Harptones, on the other hand, found their sound and rhythm in Willie Winfield's interpretation and projection and in an emotionally created harmony. Try and remember this one:

I'm through with my old love
I loved her through and through
Answer dear for a new love
Can that love be you

That's the way the group would start and in perfect harmony. Then Willie Winfield would come in:

I want a Sunday kind of love
A love to last past Saturday night
I want to know it's more than
Love at first sight

I want a Sunday kind of love
I want a love that's on the square
Can't seem to find somebody to care
I want a love to grow that leads me nowhere
I want a Sunday kind of love

The group would become very emotional:

You are my Sunday dreaming
And all my Sunday scheming
Every minute, every hour, every day
I'm hoping to discover
A certain kind of lover

The bass:

Who will show me the way

Winfield:

My heart needs someone to enfold
To keep me warm when my knees are
cold.[16]

But in each case the sound and the rhythm are distinct. One is a New York sound and the other is a Gary sound.

We were blue in the early fifties. The Second World War had ended only
a few years earlier and the Korean War was now taking away our loved ones
and splitting our groups. The automobile industry had taken those that could
not *qualify* for the war. The streets were left to those of us under fifteen years
of age. We did not know what to do with them. The effect of this street
existence changed many of our lives in our later years. It moved us towards a
materialistic approach to survival. We worshipped the automobile, the home,
the clothes, the pimp, the lawyer, the teacher, etc. Aspirations to things we
could not see or understand were viewed as strange.

Even, after the revolution of the sixties, many of our parents view our
work as strange. How can that which cannot be understood by them be
important? *When did you stray into that profession?* they ask now. Then, they
asked if it was part of the church or looked to see if white people had put an OK
on it. And the years between 1953 and now are short if you were forty years
old then. How could they grow if they were already grown? They ask (as do
many white people), how can you remember all those R & B groups and all
those songs but can't remember any of the teachers who taught you? The
question is deep if not profound. Deep in the sense that teachers did not teach
and songs and groups did as they related directly to events that we felt important. I cannot forget Clyde McPhatter and the Drifters' *Whatcha Gonna Do?*
because at the time it was popular, Ernest McNeal, Willie Jackson, and I were
caught deep in Chilli-Mac territory looking for some girls we had met at the
Madison Ballroom. As we approached the corner of Davison and Lumpkins
we heard them singing as pretty as Clyde and the Drifters themselves:

Now whatcha gonna do about half past eight
Whatcha gonna do about half past eight
It would knock me out, yes, if we had a date

You know you're so pretty/ Lawdy looka there
Yes, you're so pretty/ Lawdy looka there
Just struttin down the street/ long black wavy hair

Now, whatcha gonna say/ if I hold your hand
Whatcha gonna say/ if I hold your hand
Will you look me in my eyes/ and say I'm your lover man
Heeey aaaay aaay
Gonna reel/ gonna roll/ gonna dance/ drink
Have a ball

Whatcha gonna do about nine o' clock
Have you heard the news
Yes, we are gonna rock
(Repeat)
Yeee-aah! And never stop.

Whatcha gonna do when the joint's on fire
(Repeat)
We are gonna turn on the hose
Climb a little bit higher
Aaa-hay! Just a little bit higher
(Repeat)

We gonna keep on climbing 'til we begin to fly
Now, whatcha gonna do when the clock
Strikes four
(Repeat)
You're gonna holler, please let's
Hucklebuck some more.[17]

We were drawn over to them; forgetting that they were ass kickers. We asked them if they knew *Adorable* and *Money Honey*. They knew all the Drifters' songs. They even knew some of the routines because the group had recently appeared at the Olympia on Grand River. We sang on the corner with them for over two hours. McNeal sang lead on *Money Honey*.

Ahhh ommmmm aaah ommm
(Repeat)

You know the landlord rang my front doorbell
I let it ring a long, long spell
I went to the window, peeped through the blind
Asked him to tell me what was on his mind

He said money honey, yes money honey, money honey
If you wanna stay here with me

I was lean as a bean and so hard pressed
I called the woman I loved best
Finally I got my baby' bout half past three
She said I'd like to know what you want with me

Money honey, money honey, money honey.
She screamed and said what's wrong with me
I asked her how could another man take my place
She said money honey, money honey, money honey

Now I learned my lesson and now I know
The sun may shine and the winds may blow
The women may come and the women may go
But before I say I love 'em so,
I want money honey, money honey, money honey
If you wanna get along with me
If you wanna get along
Oh, it may sound funny
But I ain't got any money . . . [18]

We started laughing and shaking hands. Willie Jackson started right in on *Adorable:*

Adorable, adorable, adorable, adorable baby
You're so adorable, sweet as can be
You're adorable, a dream girl to me
You're all that I hope my love would ever be

You're so lovable when you're in my arms
You're so kissable when I hold your charms
You are mine
You are so divine/ adorable one

You must have come from heaven
Because you thrill me so
My heaven starts at seven sharp
You start/ my heart/ to flutter . . . [19]

As Africans, our music is sacred because it is spiritual. It has remained our common ground through three hundred years of struggle and survival in this country. No white teacher can teach this; no gang can overpower it.

The fighting groups at the time were the Shakers, the Jokers, and the Chilli-Macs. The notorious families were the Noble Brothers, the Logan Brothers, the Mitchells, the McNeal Family, the Johnson Brothers, and the French Family. Any altercation with any of them meant bloodshed. Not only were they bad, they had a reputation to uphold.

White boys were killers too. They were named Santini, Bioggi, and Cusimino. Once a thing started it was kill or be killed. The police were always on their side. They would go against the Black community while looking for the Black gang. So there were very few Black-white confrontations between families or gangs.

The Jokers would meet in Webster's Bar-B-Que joint on Mt. Elliot. The most feared of the Jokers was Tadpole. His reputation for cutting people had reached the *Michigan Chronicle*. The Lord and Master of the Shakers was Maurice. That's all anybody ever called him. He was known across the city. His number-two man was James Moody. James Moody was my friend. We met at Smith school. He lived with his mother on Joseph Campau Street until he was thirteen years old. He moved away and at sixteen he was number-two man in the Shakers. Moody was found murdered in the trunk of his Cadillac in the beginning of the seventies. I don't remember the leader of the Chilli-Macs.

Tadpole loved music as much as he loved to cut people. Every time he got money he would play the jukebox in Webster's for hours, listening to the same two records over and over again. *Smokey Joe's Cafe* by the Robins and *Play It Cool* by the Spaniels.

One day while I was eating beans
at Smokey Joe's Cafe
Just sitting digging all the scenes
at Smokey Joe's Cafe
A chick came walking through the door
That I've never seen before
At least I've never seen her down
at Smokey Joe's Cafe

And I started shakin' when she sat right down
Next to me
Her knees were almost touching mine
at Smokey Joe's Cafe
A chill was runnin' down my spine
at Smokey Joe's Cafe

I could smell the sweet perfume
She smiled at me, my heart went boom
When everybody in the room
at Smokey Joe's Cafe

They said, man, be careful that chick be-
longs to Smokey Joe.
From behind the counter/ I
saw a man/ a chef hat on his head
and a knife in his hand . . . [20]

We all would gather around the jukebox and sing along with Tadpole on the
Spaniels' record. We would harmonize in the deep *yeeeeaaAAAHHH*
ooooOOHHH Saaa-Rah!

How many more years/ will it be before
I, yes can get high/ I wanna know/ how
many more years will it be/ before I can
get high

You know, Mogen David/ jumped on a
white horse
And he beat Paul Jones/ down to Sunny
Brook.
Oh, yes, that same (k)night/ Lord Turban
got his Southern Crown.
OOOOHHH Sa-raah

I took a girl out/ the other night/ she said
whatcha want, Willie?
I said, Gimme a light!
She said, Look here, Daddy/ don't you
forget a light's no good without a
cigarette
Yes, ole Mary, she said, Willie, Willie-e-e,
Do you love me? Do you really/ Do you
really
Do you really love me . . . [21]

In the last stanza Tadpole would imitate Louis Armstrong, doing the whole
thing with the white handkerchief.

Understanding the gang, like the group, was a necessity. It was our
protection. In it we found the friends that we did not have at home. But in it we
had to prove ourselves—prove that we were men when in reality we were
boys. We would drink more wine than our enemies, drink more whiskey, and
now we must shoot more heroin. But our progression was based on material-

istic things and controlled by the same people who produce, manage, and distribute the R & B music. Why not? Were not the gangs and the groups the same people in the final analysis? After all the same Tadpole of the Jokers was the same Tadpole of the Five Dollars.

And so the Chi-Lites, the old Temptations, Smokey and the Miracles, the Dramatics, Stylistics, Delfonics, Four Tops, Black Ivory, Detroit Emeralds are rhythm and blues-ing us about the Gwen Lewises we lost years ago. Only they know us; only they can sing to us. With that rhythm we can hide the fact that we know white people are determined to control the world forever. But they can only do this by exploiting our need to survive. And by saying what we hold in our hands is just around the next corner.

Notes

[1] The Heartbeats, Rama 216.
[2] Roulette/Chess. The Pastels, Golden Goodies, Volume II.
[3] Roulette (Rama 216, Hull 720) (c) Nom Music, Inc.
[4] *Golden Teardrops* by J. Carter, Joni Music, BMI.
[5] Jubilee 5065.
[6] Jubilee 5122, by Artie Glenn (c) Valley Pub., Inc. BMI.
[7] Federal 12114.
[8] Federal 12068.
[9] Atlantic Album. *Rock Begins,* Volume 2 by Rudolph Toombs, Progressive, BMI.
[10] Atlantic 989 (*Album History of Rhythm and Blues,* Volume II) by Ahmet Ertegun, Progressive, BMI.
[11] Fortune 511 by Strong, Eubanks, Hunter, Guiterriez, Edwards, Tianon Pub., BMI.
[12] Federal 12169 by H. Ballard, Armo, BMI.
[13] Apollo 446.
[14] Federal 12046 by Johnny Otis.
[15] *Vee Jay* by C. Carter and J. Hudson, Conrad Pub. Inc., BMI.
[16] Roulette (Bruce 101) by Prima-Bell-Leonard-Rhodes, MCA Music, Inc. ASCAP.
[17] Atlantic 1005 by Ahmet Ertegun (c) by Hill and Range Music, Inc.
[18] Atlantic 1006 by Jesse Stone; Walden ASCAP, Album *Rock Begins,* Volume II.
[19] Atlantic 1078 by Buck Ram; Panther, ASCAP, Album *Rock Begins,* Volume II.
[20] Atlantic Album *Rock Begins* Volume II, Jerry Leiber and Mike Stoller; Quintet Music, BMI.
[21] *Play It Cool, Vee Jay* (Re-released on Lost Nite Album, The Spaniels 2x LP 137) Conrad (BMI).

Alive and Well and
in Your Neighborhood

IN ONE OF LANGSTON HUGHES' Simple stories, a character comes up to Simple and asks him, "How you doing, young fella?" Simple replies, "Here by the hardest, but looking forward to the best." That thought kept popping up after watching the twenty-eighth annual Tony Awards. The best play last year was a Black play and the best musical was a Black musical. A lot of nominations and three winners. It is very difficult to be a winner in the Tonys if you are Black or if you just happen to be Black. The majority of the voters are white and most of them never attend Black theatre. The seven critics who nominate are all white. Are you getting the picture? Wouldn't it be great if at least one of the critics just happened to be Black?

Best play and best musical awards for *River Niger* and *Raisin*, respectively, are the results of the explosive Black theatre movement of the early sixties and the highly controversial concepts of its practitioners. We who are responsible for it know that many side effects are now apparent, i.e., Black films, television, publishing... Those who are capitalizing on it say the two are not related. All Black art is relative: let's look and see what we can see, and most surely if we can see we will learn.

The Black theatre movement is almost ten years old now, and we who tried so hard to make it happen, suffered mentally and financially, always knew, that out there Black people existed who would support us by their presence if we gave them Blackness. We *made* the Black theatre movement happen for the greater good of theatre in this country—just as Black people made the Black Power movement happen against all odds. First, we put it in the consciousness of the people. We forced it into the university system via student unions and Black study programs. We made it a common media term. Black playwrights began to write exclusively for Black theatres. Black actors and directors became better trained by performing before the discriminating eye of Black people. And Black people began to demand more from their playwrights, actors, and directors.

In the early sixties we began honing our artistic instruments. Some of us came out of the woodshed with instruments ready and thinking that the American way of the good artist is Off-Broadway — Broadway; on to television and films with each stop being a benchmark. But, alas, that is the white American way.

It has nothing to do with the Black theatre movement. Black writers are not being considered when Hollywood tries to produce Black art. Don't you ask yourself sometimes why *The Invisible Man* and *Go Tell It on the Mountain* are not transferred to film? Why *No Place to Be Somebody, Ceremonies in Dark Old Men, In the Wine Time, Slaveship, The Black Terror* are not transferred to film? Well, ask yourself that question. For years we were angry because Blacks would not invest in the Black theatre movement. Recently we have begun to realize that money from foundations and the government are equally due to Black culture. It is as much ours as it is Lincoln Center's or Kennedy Center's. Yet, we must constantly beg for it. In some cases we are directed to wealthy Black Americans (Sidney Poitier, Sammy Davis, etc.). But those few Blacks who are pretending riches, imitating the Fords, the Rockefellers, and the Kennedys are not responsible. Individually the Fords, the Rockefellers, Kennedys are not responsible for white American art. Those few Blacks cannot give away what they honestly do not have. They do not have any money individually. What they have is *collective* wealth and an image of singular wealth. That singular image might be needed on an opening night but that's the extent of that participation. However, collectively, any ten of the wealthy Blacks could get the money to produce the whole Black theatre movement.

Since the middle sixties Black energy has been instrumental in serving the American theatre. The American theatre had been invaded with European theatre. We came to know it as theatre of the absurd, theatre of the angry young men, and theatre of the avant-garde. White writers began to copy this movement and American theatre became what could be called a bad imitation. White people could not deal with it; they started looking for innovative and fresh theatre. Some found excitement in Black theatre as they had found in jazz music because it refused to address itself to them directly. They could sit and watch (peek in) but they could not control its direction.

Did you know that those institutions and individuals most instrumental in forging the Black theatre movement are still the controlling force in it? Vinnette Carroll, Free Southern Theatre, Concept-East, Amiri Baraka, Woodie King, Ron Milner, Ed Bullins, Douglas Turner Ward, Robert Hooks, Elma Lewis, Barbara Ann Teer, the late great Langston Hughes, and all those Black

people who heard the chant of the new Black poets telling them how beautiful
Black is. Some of us are successful and some of us are not, but all of us are
unhappy at what we see. White institutions are trying to define our art through
federal and foundation support which we should be getting. In some cases we
are rejected because we are political; yet all art is political. In other cases we
are rejected because we are not relevant to the community; yet the community
is wherever Black people are—and they are everywhere. The media has
silenced our Black critics by not hiring them. The white critics see our work as
being irrelevant, and they are right. Our work is irrelevant to their life-style.

Yet, the Black theatre persists; it exists. We know if there had been no
Black theatre movement there would have been no Black movies to help save
that dying industry and no Negro Ensemble Company to produce the best play
last year. There probably would have been no Lonnie Elders or Joseph Walk-
ers or Ron Milners or J.E. Franklins. So, you see, the struggle has been for
the greater good.

Now in the mid-seventies we need Black cultural institutions on the level
of Lincoln Center, Mark Taper Forum, and the Kennedy Center. The Black
institutions could even be an imitation—it doesn't matter. What matters is, in
a country where twenty-five million Blacks live and breathe, there is no
cultural institution for them. This is unbelievable when one thinks about it.
We can complain about the white institutions but they exist now and they will
continue to exist. They will program us with their art, music, theatre and
dance and they will do it better than most of the short-lived, ill-equipped,
under-financed Black projects. We need these institutions immediately if our
art is to survive.

The seventies haven't been very good to the Black theatre movement.
Remember back in 1970 when all those Blacks who had supported the sixties
started putting down all Black theatre? Some even denied their own Blackness. I do recall in 1971 a lot of Blacks seemed happy that the Negro Ensemble
Company was in financial trouble. Most of us remember 1972 as the year the
Black theatre received so few grants, so little support; the Black press called
any play with more than half of its performers Black, Black theatre. Many
Black artists went into white institutions not only teaching Black art to white
students but rejecting the Black values that caused them to be hired in the first
place. On the West Coast, Blacks want an integrated experience. No one
wants to hear Black pride talk. *Everyone is just people.* Yet whites control the
media, images and imagination. Therefore, they control the magic—the
money. And money seems to be controlling those Blacks on the West Coast.

The Black theatre movement must avoid this internal conflict. And it must secure Black artists in its ranks who will give to it rather than take from it. It is no secret that white people will pay for the control of the Black theatre movement. I will say here as I've said before, the Black theatre movement cannot support its artists as well as the white theatre movement supports its artists until Black people *see* Black theatre as a reflection of themselves. At the present time, a Black producer producing Black theatre does not get the same return on the dollar as his white counterpart. From theatre rentals to advertising rates in news media, the Black theatre suffers because costs are based on what white people are able to pay for a seat. The media is also effective at reaching those same white people. Black artists must be reminded of this. Blacks on Broadway in *River Niger* and *Raisin* are missionaries while those in *Pippin* and *Over Here* laborers.

The Black theatre movement doesn't have Lonnie Elder *(Ceremonies in Dark Old Men)*, Douglas Turner Ward *(Day of Absence* and *Happy Ending)*. James Baldwin *(Amen Corner* and *Blues for Mister Charlie)*. Charles Gordone *(No Place to Be Somebody)*, or Ossie Davis *(Purlie Victorious)* writing for it anymore. However, it does have some innovative and new playwrights who must be supported by our presence and our understanding: Ed Bullins, Ron Milner, Joseph Walker, Richard Wesley, J.E. Gaines, Martie Evans-Charles, J.E. Franklin, Leslie Lee, Walter Jones, Edgar White, Paul Carter Harrison, Phillip Hayes Dean, and Charles Fuller are but a few out of the seventies. They will certainly capture the Black life-style in beautiful and artistic form. Joseph Walker did it with *River Niger* and Ron Milner did it with *What the Winesellers Buy*. Milner and Walker did not just happen overnight. If we open our eyes we will see small ill-equipped black-controlled theatre across the country. All of them need us to support their efforts (thank you, Bette Midler!). I mentioned some of them earlier and I mention them again: Free Southern Theater, Concept-East, Spirit House Movers, Negro Ensemble Company, New Federal Theatre, National Black Theatre, D.C. Black Repertory, Afro-American Studio, Black Arts West, Inner City of Los Angeles, and the Black Theatre Alliance of New York. Remember the names! These theatres are developing writers, technicians, and audiences for Broadway. And they will be in the arena helping to save Broadway. It is important that the Tony Awards give credit where and when it is due. It is not doing that now because it is now a fraternity of white people.

New York is Not the Answer

An interview by the late Hoyt W. Fuller
from *Black World,* April 1975.

You are known as a director, producer, actor, film director, editor, anthologist and organizer of poetry festivals. Is there a single, underlying thread which holds together all these interests?

I see myself as someone who works in the arts. All the arts are presentational and all must be directed to Black people. Most Black people are basically the same. In other words, those watching have a common understanding since all are oppressed in one way or the other. The thread that holds it all together is the audience.

Will the advocates of true Black theatre eventually have to reject the lure and tenets of Broadway—as some Black theatre groups already have done—in order to realize their full potential as artists and also in order to maintain their personal and artistic integrity?

Definitely! Broadway is New York and I don't feel Black theatre has much of a chance in New York. The lure and the temptation of success is everywhere, and a Black artist who has been suffering for years can witness the overnight successes of his associates. Most artists might talk Black but when it comes to signing contracts they want you to make them Edward Albee or Robert Redford. They don't realize that the people who pay to see them assume they are Willie Best or Flip Wilson. A Black theatre institution can only survive outside of New York. I said "institution" where a lot of Black artists can produce and work—not one-man operations that end when that particular individual goes on to riches and fame.

Do you feel that genuine Black theatre ultimately will have to depend on Black audiences?

It has been doing that. White people won't go to Black theatre unless it becomes the in thing. We know "in" changes for white people from year to year. The expense accounts and the theatre parties from Jewish America don't go to Black theatre. Those Blacks who do go view it as a smaller version of white art. Blacks don't view it, as of this writing, as something that should cost $15 per ticket. But those in it know that it costs me the same to produce a Black play on Broadway as it costs David Merrick to produce a white play.

Given the economic realities of Broadway theatre and the special "dissident" character of Black theatre, what do you see as the prospects for the development of viable and financially stable Black theatrical productions?

Black performing artists cannot expect to have financial returns equal to white artists unless they are going to perform before a white audience. By that I mean, Ben Vereen in *Pippin* is different from, say, Glynn Turman in *What the Winesellers Buy,* because *Pippin* is a white show even though the lead is Black. The audience for *Pippin* is almost totally white. It is aimed at a white audience. A stable theatrical production aimed at a Black audience must seek out those artists who are interested in that kind of theatre and proceed without benefit of those white unions and other white values that have been destroying Black people from the day one. First, that cannot happen in New York under the present conditions. Not complaining, but it should not cost a Black producer the same to produce a Black play as it cost his white counterparts to produce a white play. Ticket costs, advertising rates, theatre rental, and so on, are based on what a white person can afford to pay for a ticket.

How is the dilemma to be resolved between a Black theatre which speaks against the norms and values of a consumer-capitalist American society, and the need to appeal for support to that society in order to succeed both artistically and financially on Broadway?

It is not to be resolved on Broadway or in that tradition. Until Black people feel a need to support Black theatre, Black theatre will be functioning at odds with itself. I've said this often enough, and I'll say it again: Black people just might view James Brown and Al Green as our Black theatre because we all know Black people are supporting them. The realities of it all seem to be—if the dollars going out do not equal the dollars coming in, we must do what is necessary to equalize that. I know that's a strange statement, but as a commercial producer I must ask myself those questions or I will not be able to protect Black investors who support Black theatre. As a producer I cannot continue to risk Black money when I know it might not be returned.

What — if any — are the changes in the Black-theatre-going population since you produced A Black Quartet *several years ago?*

I think more Black people went to the theatre then because it cost a lot less to see a play. Also, there weren't that many plays on, and students found more interest because it seemed to be a new form of protest. At *A Black Quartet* we had bus loads of students from all over the state led by energetic young Black teachers or liberal white ones. We all know that has changed. The seventies cry that all the Black energy was wasted or, as Dr. Richard Long puts it: The sixties are getting blamed for all the crap of the seventies. Even the writers of those four one-act plays changed their politics four or five times since then.

Do you have a producing company? What is it called?

I work for the Henry Street Settlement. In 1970 I formed the New Federal Theater there. It's really an offshoot of Mobilization For Youth. MFY, as it was called, was a training program for young people that was very successful during the sixties. The New Federal does seven plays per year on a workshop scale.

Is the probability of freedom of statement greater in Black films than in Black theatre?

It depends on who one is working for. I've personally never had any problems with freedom of statement. I found problems with getting money. We all know in film and theatre that once one gets the financing he does what he wants to do. But there is one great thing about film: once the statement is made, it is made forever.

What are some of the film projects you would like to undertake?

Well, right now I am editing Julian Mayfield's *The Long Night.* I expect it to be in the theatres in mid-1975. I am also planning the film version of *What the Winesellers Buy. Harlem Transfer,* a film based on Evan Walker's short story, is also in the works.

How did you raise the funds to produce your first full-length film, The Long Night?

I went out to Black people as always and explained what we were trying to do. Then I brought in Ed Pitt as associate producer and St. Clair Bourne as co-producer. Now it is a joint project. On that same basis I was able to get performers like Dick Williams, Peggy Kirkpatrick, Geoffrey King, Sunny Jim Gaines, Shauneille Perry, etc. All good people whom I've worked with before. Roger Furman even helped get people for me.

How much money must the film make before the investors and the author will have a profit?
Somewhere in the area of half-a-million dollars.

Are you satisfied with the arrangements you had to make in order to get national distribution for your film?
No... Well, it would be very simple if I could go from city to city and distribute my own film, but economics make that almost impossible. Theatre owners want films that are big and corny because they feel that's what Black people want.

Please comment on problems of production, funding and distribution of Black films.
Funding and distribution are the main problems. Productions vary with the individuals who are in charge. Everyone starts out to make a good product but some can verbalize their artistic intent better than others, some can put that intent on film better than verbalize it... but distribution is the problem. Very few Blacks own film theatres or distribution companies. The money comes into the theatre and goes to the distributor before it comes to the producer. Therein is where the rip-off occurs. On a fair count, if a ticket costs $3, the theatre owner keeps $1.25, he sends $1.75 to the distributor. The distributor pays for prints, advertising, promotion, and everything else he can, and sends the producer the rest after he deducts 30 percent. If the producer is lucky, he will get $.50. Out of that he must pay back his investors and all those performers who think they are the Robert Redfords or Faye Dunaways.

Did you find wealthy Black Americans who were interested in investing in your film?
Wealthy Black Americans, I am sorry to say, do not invest. Wealthy Black Americans invest in AT&T or Twentieth Century-Fox.

What are the names of the poetry records you have produced?
Amiri Baraka's *Nation Time, Blackspirits: New Black Poets in America,* and *Forerunners.*

How have they sold?

They were not promoted so they didn't sell. What I found to be the case with record companies, they don't have the know-how or the personnel to promote. If the distributor isn't interested, the record is dropped. Another problem, poetry records won't sell in record shops.

What are the names of the anthologies you have edited?

Black Quartet (NAL), *Poets and Prophets* (NAL), *Black Drama Anthology* (with Ron Milner, NAL), *Blackspirits* (Random House), *Black Short Story Anthology* (NAL), and *Forerunners* (Howard University Press).

How have they sold?

Not good according to what the white boys tell me, but everywhere we go someone has a copy.

Do you see the Black Theater Alliance (BTA) as a potential force ensuring larger audiences and increased financial support for Black theatre?

The Black Theatre Alliance is a one-woman operation. So far, it explains Black theatre to white people. On a small scale I've been able to get what I want for New Federal. It's probably because Joan Sandler, Director of BTA, is a very good friend. None of us, however, demands from the Alliance those things that it was set up to give. I think it is because we all know the difficulties of just paying the rent. But on the whole, an organization will have difficulties helping others if it can't support itself.

Do you feel that Black theatre might achieve significant "breakthroughs" in some locality removed from the pressures and influences of Broadway?

That's what I was trying to say earlier about New York and Broadway. For Black theatre to survive it has to be removed from the financial temptations of New York and Broadway. As a matter of fact, I know of no successful Black business in New York.

What are some of your plans and projects for the immediate future?

Well...I mentioned the film projects. For the stage I will be touring *Prodigal Sister,* a musical by J.E. Franklin and Mikki Grant. *What the Winesellers Buy* will probably have played Chicago by the time this is in print. Also, Ed Bullins' *The Fabulous Miss Marie* will be touring the United States. It will be directed by Robert Macbeth. At New Federal Theater, I am producing Ed Bullins' *The Taking of Miss Janie.* It's directed by Gil Moses. Next will be Piri Thomas' *Saturday Night*. I will end the season with Amiri Bara-ka directing his new play, *The Kid Poet, Heroic*. All in all, I expect lots of excitement because I have put people together who would otherwise not even speak to each other. For me that's what's so exciting about working in the Black theatre movement.

The Prodigal Sister cast, New York City, 1974. Neal Tate, music director (left); Micki Grant, composer; and Shauneille Perry, director.

How Winesellers *Came to the Stage: Log of a Hit*

THERE HAD BEEN TIMES, back in Detroit in the early sixties, when Hasting Street existed in our reality so clearly, so precisely, that we never dreamed that in the early seventies it would be the subject of a playwright's homage—at a time when we could not even visit it again. Now we must remember. We must place it in the reality of today. Hasting Street existed in our youth not as a ghetto but as home. The people in our home must be honored as we remember them. The decisions we made because of some remembered statement. There had been times when we did not know "what the winesellers bought [was] one-half so precious as what they sold." My friend, Ron Milner, tried to make us see that again in his play, *What the Winesellers Buy.*

When I received the play in October of 1972, exactly two years had passed since Ron Milner had last sent me a play. I read it in one night; decided to sit on it for a week; and then read it again. After the second reading I called him and told him I wanted to do it. Nothing emotional, nothing heavy. He said, "Fine," I asked him to apply for a Rockefeller grant to come into New York to work on it with me at the New Federal Theater. He received the grant and became the writer-in-residence as of January 1973. Milner and I understand each other. He never sends me a play unless it's ready. I never ask him to do anything unless I know it can be done.

First, I took the play to the Negro Ensemble Company (NEC). I always feel more objective on works I like and usually let other artists guide me, which has been a weakness for years. So, because of my feeling for the play and my feeling for the NEC, I felt the two should be together. But the NEC decided the play wasn't for them. Next, on one rainy night Ron and I took it to my partner, Dick Anthony Williams. We talked in general about hustlers and the Rico character, knowing all the while we wanted Dick to play the role. Dick was cool. He rapped, letting us know he knew as much about "the life" as we did. When Dick called a few days later and said he would do it, we scheduled rehearsals at Henry Street Settlement's New Federal Theater for April 1973. Each day of rehearsals something new about the old Detroit neighborhood loomed before me. Both Ron and I became obsessed with a kind of precision that's not found in most Black plays. Most of the cast were from places like Detroit, Cleveland and Chicago. We wanted the Midwest sound: the slight musical tone in the mothers; not the tone of old mothers, but the quality of Black women who mothered children in their teens. Mothers in their mid-thirties. A rhythm not present in most New York actors. If all these small pointers were to be accomplished, then we had to work at least as hard as the performers trying to achieve them. Ron wrote and rewrote daily. He cut, edited, changed words. My directorial problems were difficult. I saw the whole play as a motion picture. The set itself had to be five playing areas. Charles Mills created a series of spaces with $800 that would have sent more experienced designers back to the drawing board. Moving the performers from one space to the next as fast as the lights could go up and out would be the style. All movements would be geometric. This movement, with the help of Dick Anthony Williams, a director in his own right, at times reached poetic heights. I also used simultaneous and overlapping actions.

Costumes, I felt, would be the most important. Judy Dearing, who had costumed dancers in the Ailey Company, was selected as designer. We talked of costumes so much that at times I felt embarrassed. What I wanted was not a fit, but a look. I wanted Rico, the pimp, to look like a lean, high fashion model. That look had been captured only once, and that was on a real life hustler on *Black Journal,* the television show. I even tried to get a tape of the show for the designer.

The crucial decision had to be the direction of the two teen-agers, Steve and Mae. It had to be a play about the choice Black teens must make at so early an age. Therefore, the Rico character had to be very real, he had to be believable at all times. For a young person to make the right choice against such convincing odds demanded of the play solid structure and a most positive sense of the subtle dynamics of the Black community. Some critic called *What the Winesellers Buy* a morality play. I don't see any problems in that. We are a moral people. White people fear any kind of morality; they are not moral, generally. Ron Milner created Rico in the images of the white world. All his values had been learned from watching the white world. Every statment, though hidden in Black rhythm, is based on a white value system. I think Rico is one of the most fascinating Black characters in contemporary Black literature. At one point he tells Steve, ''There are only two kinds of people in this world; those standing around trembling, waiting to be told when and how to move, and those with guts enough to jump in and tell them *when* and *how!*''

A strong Black man, Jim Aron, figures in the drama as a friend of the mother. It is apparent he is to be the adversary of Rico. He talks to young Steve about life and how a man manages and exists. He is a deacon in the church where Steve's mother has retreated after Steve's father's death. The author brings in the influence of the Black church. My directing on this section was designed to move the audience's attention from the preachiness of the deacon's words to the young man. Therefore, the selection of the performer had to be *against the type.* In theatre sometimes we cast a play to type. It can be very dangerous for a drama for an audience to get ahead of the story by knowing too much about the characters prematurely. We selected a street-wise performer named Bill Cobbs. He could easily have played Rico on another level. When they stood face to face, it was difficult for an audience to side with either. Again, this left the choice up to the teen-ager, Steve: When the deacon tells Steve, ''Wanna know what a man is, don't look at his car, his clothes, his bank account, look at his woman. Whatever he is will be right there in her. If she's a whore, then he is a whore too. . . .'' Directing a character to listen to the truth of another character takes much time and patience. Often the actors playing the roles must spend time together away from rehearsals. Bill Cobbs and Herb Rice (Steve) got together often as did Dick Anthony Williams and Herb Rice. I would be with them for little meetings over coffee or at other plays. Those four and one half weeks of rehearsals became a lifetime.

Directing is only manipulating the truth and getting ten or fifteen performers to understand that truth. Actors need to believe that what they are doing, the characters they are portraying, are deep and profound when in reality they are not. In directing *What the Winesellers Buy,* I had to make the performers understand the Black people they portrayed; to make them understand that the characters were *Black* and not out of white American literature. Blocking actors, moving them about a stage, is no easy task. Few directors ever talk about it because each play has its own set of demands. Pacing a play about the Black life-style can be done with simple devices like music, voice rhythm, and style. I used music and style in the pacing of *Winesellers.* Voice rhythm was already there so clear and precise from the first reading that I never had to deal with it. The truth of the mother's character, at times, I missed. Sometimes I could not find words to explain exactly what Ron Milner wanted. Looking back on it, I feel it was so well defined in the writing that any woman who had lived in a Black community and who had birthed children would understand. But I did not observe the old lesson Lloyd Richards taught me: never assume. For me, bringing the role of the mother to life on stage was most difficult. Some fine actresses have played it; yet in the end I always feel something missing. Juanita Clark, a fine actress from Detroit, brought the role closer to a reality for me when she played it on tour. However, I don't feel it was my direction. It was a Detroit rhythm and truth that I can't explain but which I know when I see it and hear it.

You will note that I've deliberately stayed away from theories, practices, time, space . . . Stanislavski, etc. Knowing one's craft as a director or actor at this time in our history is a prerequisite for any kind of understanding. There's no excuse for not knowing. When one says he is an actor or a writer, I don't question him. I might not agree on what he has written or the way he portrays a character, but I won't disagree with his right to do it the way he is doing it. Milner knows the rules, therefore he has the right to violate them. The performers selected for the premiere production of the *Winesellers* were 99 percent correct. Directing them was a joy, no matter how difficult; they were good craftsmen from the beginning to the end. Directing *Winesellers* forced me to remember those people in the Detroit that I grew up in. I am sure the personal feelings I brought to the project could have hurt the play had I not had the author at most of the rehearsals. As I am trying to keep theories and practices out of this article, I tried to keep those discussions out of rehearsals. Milner's presence helped me to do that.

Act One had to be concerned with creating a feeling for that area of our ghetto that was Hasting Street. The people had to be clear; they had to be introduced correctly. Everything had to tie into the need for material things, money being the basic need. Act Two had to show to what ends Black people must go in order to survive. Act Three had to show the moral philosophy Black people must follow no matter what the condition. In short, each act of *What the Winesellers Buy* led me to these conclusions as a director.

What the Winesellers Buy opened in May 1973. All the reviews were average. The Black audience loved it. We played weekends, Thursday through Sunday. Inspired by the response of the audiences, Milner continued to rewrite. Each new rewrite helped the play. At times Milner would deliver rewrites on one day and I would include them the next day. What started out as a three-and-one-half hour play was cut to three hours by the time the play closed at the New Federal Theater. Loretta Greene, the actress who played Mae, the young heroine, received so many rewrites that she eventually lost her voice for three days. However, like the trouper that she is, she went into the hospital on Monday and returned to play the role on Thursday. Most actresses could not cope under those circumstances. Ms. Greene, however, had played other Milner characters in *A Black Quartet*. She had also co-starred in my production of *Black Girl*. In many of the plays that I've produced or directed, performers and writers generally are too lazy to put in the kind of work that good literature demands. Because of the turn-away audiences, the play was held over two weekends. When it finally closed in June 1973, I immediately set out to produce it and direct it as an independent.

Meanwhile, I was able to get a production in Los Angeles through Michael Schultz. Michael had not seen my production but he had heard about it. He had an arrangement with Gordon Davidson at the Theater For Now series of the Mark Taper Forum. The production opened in Los Angeles in October 1973. Milner did even more rewrites out there. He finally had the kind of performer he worked well with in Glynn Turman. Glynn had played the hero in Milner's *Who's Got His Own* in New York in 1966. Back in New York I was setting up backers' auditions and trying to raise the $85,000 to do it Off-Broadway. One of the backers I tried to pull in was Joseph Papp, via Bernie Gersten. Papp liked the play and said he wanted it to be the first Black play on the Beaumont Theater stage in Lincoln Center. He did not see the production that I directed at the New Federal Theater, but he had seen Michael Schultz's direction. He said he would produce it if Michael directed. Michael did not want to take a directing job away from me, and Milner felt since I had done it first I should do it at the Beaumont. But I love Michael's work so I sat Milner and Schultz down in Hollywood and convinced them to do the play. Papp agreed that I would be the associate producer. That way I would see how producing is done on a larger scale. Papp and I pulled (together) the best elements of the two productions and went into rehearsals in December 1973 with a budget of $200,000. In January, 1974, while the play rehearsed in Philadelphia, Milner made another major rewrite. He changed the ending. Rico would not get killed by the police as in the original script. Rico would be a continuing menace to the Black community. Milner felt that he had taken the weight off Steve by killing off Rico.

The play opened in New York at the Vivian Beaumont Theater in January 1974. It closed March 17, 1974. It made more money for Lincoln Center than Papp's other three productions. Papp decided it was the kind of production he wanted for his touring summer productions. He asked me to direct it. This involved another rewrite. Milner cut the play to ninety minutes. We went into rehearsals in June. *Winesellers* toured the Manhattan, Bronx, Queens, and Brooklyn parks in July and August, 1974. This is also the production that later toured the country. But again I had an opportunity to use all the performers from the original production at the New Federal Theater. Directional changes were at a minimum, although technical changes were necessary because now there would be no intermission. (In the original production, there had been two intermissions. In the touring version we used only one intermission.) All these are minor changes and all are customary in developing any production.

A major problem, however, was Papp's refusal to deal with the play as a commercial property after he had seen the way Black people reacted to its message. I decided I would not be caught again in the position I found myself after the Beaumont production, unable to move on with the play as a commercial property. Halfway through the summer tour, I arranged a co-production with Moe Septee in Philadelphia. We opened in November, 1974; that tour continued through November, 1975, and plans were made to present *What the Winesellers Buy* on Broadway.

Gloria Edwards (left), Lyn Whitfield, and Charlie Brown in *Showdown,* New York City, 1976.

We Must Sustain
Our Own Theatres

An interview by Barbara Lewis
from *Black Theatre Alliance Newsletter,* November 1977.

VERY FEW PRODUCERS IN
the nonprofit theatre make personal money on any show. The fact that I did
Colored Girls means that I can add another production to the season. And I'm
guaranteed my job a little longer,'' remarks Woodie King, Jr., the Black
producer who first developed *For Colored Girls Who Have Considered
Suicide/ When The Rainbow is Enuf* before Joseph Papp took it to Broadway.

We were sitting in his long and narrow office lined with plaques, posters,
and awards at Henry Street Settlement, the cultural complex at the southern tip
of Manhattan where he founded the New Federal Theatre seven years ago.
Presiding over an average of five productions annually and serving as a
consultant for many others, King's decisions affect the course and flow of
Black theatre in New York and across the country. *Colored Girls* has gener-
ated albums, T-shirts, a California cast; the book was recently published by
Macmillan, and the road company has a contract through the summer of 1978.
Apart from co-production billing, Woodie King receives nothing, but Henry
Street as the sponsoring theatre receives a percentage of the return. This is a
bracing insight on the position of the Black producer on Broadway, and more
generally on the condition of the Black arts. As a commercial venture, Black
theatre is too often siphoned off from the Black community where it
originated.

The gateway to a flourishing future for the arts hinges on the Black
audience. Ultimately, we must support and sustain our own theatres indepen-
dently. With that premise in mind, King began to produce films, record
albums, mount plays, write and edit books, all to widen exposure for Black
cultural endeavors.

Herbert Rice and Loretta Green in *What the Winesellers Buy,* New York, 1973

A significant force behind the Black literary renaissance of the sixties, King helped to sow the seeds for the current expansion in Black writing. At heart a writer who has penned numerous short stories, feature articles and several screenplays, King has a sensibility for the timeless. As an editor, King compiled the short stories of the leading Black writers and in collaboration with playwright Ron Milner collected the best of the new Black plays in *Black Drama Anthology* (1970). One year later, King sponsored a three-day festival, "New Black Poets in America," which he held in three key places: Harlem, Brooklyn and Newark. *The Long Night,* a sepia-toned feature film released by King and his co-producer, St. Clair Bourne, in 1975, was selected for showing at the Moscow Film Festival in August. The rambunctious Last Poets of Harlem were the subject of King's prize-winning documentary, *Right On!* As theatre producer, King stood behind such productions as *A Black Quartet* (four one-act plays by Amiri Baraka, Ed Bullins, Ben Caldwell, and Ron Milner), *Slaveship* (Baraka), *Jamimma* (Martie Evans-Charles), *Cotillion* (John Killens), *The Taking of Miss Janie* (Bullins), *Black Girl* (J. E. Franklin) and *What the Winesellers Buy* (Ron Milner), giving exposure to Black writers not ardently courted by the public or press. Woodie King's reputation has crested on the wave of this onrush of new playwrights.

Woodie King was born in Mobile, Alabama. When he was five, the family moved to Detroit. Several years later he began appearing in commercials. His senior year in high school, King received a scholarship to the prestigious Will-O-Way School, earning an undergraduate degree in theatre in 1961. Woodie King began piling up credits as a producer of new playwrights while enrolled at Wayne State University in Michigan. A group of actors, spearheaded by King, felt they were being discriminated against in the distribution of roles, and were not given sufficient opportunities to display and stimulate their craft. With the backing of the NAACP, they founded the Concept-East Theatre in 1962.

"We took a bar and remade it inside. It was like a cabaret but it had 100 seats in it. We did five or six plays a year. We produced both Black and white playwrights: Baraka, Bullins, Milner, Edward Albee, Jack Gelber and Rev. Malcolm Boyd," remembered King.

At the Concept-East, King learned everything about running a theatre, about ledger sheets, about balancing the books, putting up the lights, stage managing a production. Having to do it all, he became adept and thorough at taking a project from inception to maturity. And simultaneously, he continued his career as an actor and director, touring the country with productions from the Concept- East.

Ron Milner, author of *What the Winesellers Buy.*

Coming out of Detroit in 1964, Woodie King arrived in New York in time to add his flame to the fire of revolutionary intensity that Bullins, Baraka, Stokely Carmichael and the Black Panther Party were fomenting. The term, "Black theatre," although far from new, had just been sanctioned by *Newsweek* and federal funding was abundant.

"All the niggers you see out there working now including myself and all these Black theatres got the money because the people who had the money were trying to stop Baraka. They would do anything they could to balance him out, they gave money to Bob Macbeth at New Lafayette to stop Baraka. Baraka made all of it possible because he was raising so much hell, picketing everybody. You saw more Black people on television during that period. As soon as it quieted down, you didn't see that anymore."

His first year in New York, King co-founded Theatre Genesis, an Off-Off-Broadway house in the Church of St. Mark's-in-The-Bowery, and was also involved with the American Place Theatre during its early days at St. Clements Church. Awarded a John Hay Whitney fellowship, King studied directing with Lloyd Richards, the Black director who staged the original Broadway production of *Raisin in the Sun,* and theater administration with Wynn Handman, executive director of the American Place Theatre. At the end of his apprenticeship at American Place, King began to resume his interest in producing.

"The kinds of plays that I wanted to do weren't going to get done unless I produced them, plays that Black actors could be important in rather than peripheral."

In 1965, King designed a federally sponsored cultural training program at Mobilization for Youth on the lower East Side. "We made films, we sent young people to Paris and Rome to perform. Playwrights E. Franklin, Lonnie Elder, and Douglas Turner Ward were some of the writers. I paid people more than they had ever been paid. Everyone thought it was going to be a fly-by-night but it proved very successful."

Five years later, the training program was incorporated into the New Federal Theatre, under the auspices of the Henry Street Settlement. Based on the old Federal Theatre, a Harlem unit funded by the government from 1935 to 1939, King maintained a tradition of free quality theatre.

Last season, King departed slightly from precedent by charging admission for two of the productions at New Federal: a much-touted revival of the Haitian version of *Macbeth* (popular at the old Federal Theatre) and Ron Milner's a capella musical, *Season's Reasons.* Edgar White's political commentary on West Indians in America, *The Defense,* was the initial offering.

Right on its heels came *The Divine Comedy,* Owen Dodson's poetic dirge of futility and redemption. Next Soledad presented *Perdido,* her lament for a wayward generation of Puerto Rican men. Ed Bullins' epic play *Daddy* played to packed houses and may soon find its way to a larger theatre with Woodie King as producer.

Given the circumstances of American theatre at this point on Broadway, King is readily accepting slots as a director, most recently staging Elaine Jackson's play *Cockfight* at the American Place Theatre. "I am directing more than I am producing because there are so many Black plays on Broadway being produced by white people for white audiences. And the plays, no matter how Black in intention, will be absorbed by a white theatre-going audience rather than a Black audience. The Black audiences are so happy to see Black people on stage that they don't deal with who produced it. In the plays directed by Black people, the content is controlled a little bit more." On this crucial issue, the Black Theatre Alliance, King feels, can be a decisive factor influencing "the attitudes of the New York theatre-going public."

Presently completing his most ambitious film project to date, King received several grants last winter, including one from the American Film Institute and another from the National Endowment for the Arts (for which the Black Theatre Alliance acted as a conduit) to produce and direct a documentary chronicling the national emergence of Black theatre. Dating back to 1959 when Lorraine Hansberry's *Raisin In the Sun* captured the Best Play of The Year from the Drama Critics Circle, the film will be a "precise history of the Black theatre movement," culled from interviews with noted personalities and footage of both current and historical plays.

Defining the Black Theatre Alliance as "one of the most important organizations to come to the aid of Black theatre, providing services that would take us individually a long time to be able to muster," King, one of the first members of the Alliance, concluded: "The Black Theatre Alliance has not taken any kind of revolutionary steps in dealing with the constraints that white theatre now holds over the New York theatre scene. As an organization, the BTA has the power to do that."

How the Movement
Got Started

THE AMERICAN BLACK THEATRE movement: Dateline '77. What is it? Where is it going? And why? I just want to start by saying that it's alive and I think it's everywhere. I think it's everywhere because of forerunners like the Karamu Theatre, Langston Hughes, Canada Lee, and the American Negro Theatre. I think because of those people and libraries where we can go and read about those people, we are able to see that past, to know some of the things that had gone on before and not be too afraid to try some things ourselves. Before I actually went into theatre I spent more time in the library looking for photographs of Blacks in theatre than I spent in school. So when I got to the point of deciding whether I really wanted to go into theatre, it really didn't matter too much where I got the training because I had a certain kind of history of what came before me that would guide me.

The Black theatre movement started for me in 1961-62 in Detroit at a place called the Concept-East Theatre which I founded with Ron Milner, David Rambeau, and some other brothers. We all got together with a thousand dollars; we all put up a hundred dollars each. There were no foundations at that time. One of the things we found out very early was that a one-man operation is impossible in the Black theatre structure as it exists. At that time we found you had to know how to direct, how to make sets and lights. Everybody had to know how to do everything. Running that little theatre in Detroit was a great learning experience.

When I came to New York, I found that few Black people were actually involved in running theatres, when there were bars and churches everywhere vacant. Cliff Frazier and I set out to start a theatre. It's funny because we went to a place just two blocks from here called the Church of St. Mark's-in-the-Bowery and asked the minister if we could have the parish hall to do some plays. We started a theatre called Theatre Genesis in 1963-64. I think it's still going on. We did our own plays.

So one of the things we learned very early was one man cannot totally run a theatre in New York and be totally successful with it because the system has ways of cutting him down.

Another thing about Black theatre I keep running into is that we fail to develop directors. I don't know what we can do about it. I think the Frank Silvera Writers' Workshop actually has a director's workshop. I know our theatre is developing them. We do six or seven plays a year and I try to get as many different directors coming in as possible to work on plays; it gives the theatre a different personality. I think when a theatre takes on one personality it's a problem. This is one of our errors. We should try to do something about it as soon as possible.

Another problem is we have not distinguished what the Black theatre movement was really about in the early sixties. For me it came out of some work Baraka was doing up in Harlem and down here at the Saint Mark's Playhouse. Right after that he went uptown and started the Black Arts Repertory Theatre and wrote a position paper called "Revolutionary Black Theatre: What It's All About," which was very inspiring to me. That paper, and that feeling in Harlem helped, indirectly, a great many Blacks across the country to get over. The white establishment was so afraid of Baraka they would do anything. They would just give money away. Anybody who said they didn't like Baraka got a grant.

What we failed to do, though, was distinguish what Black theatre is. I know right now a white person buying a ticket for *Guys and Dolls* and *Brownsville Raid* sees both of these pieces of work as Black theatre. He doesn't see any difference in paying $12 for *Guys and Dolls* and $6.95 for *Brownsville Raid*. He wants *Brownsville Raid* to be just as flashy and full of music as *Guys and Dolls* because he wants to be entertained.

In trying to get the word out, to get the Black theatre movement out before the public, we did not make that distinction. We did not distinguish that "something" for a lot of Black people. I believe that my mother or a lot of our mothers would come in to New York and go see *Hello, Dolly!* on Broadway and go and see *Unfinished Women* and deal with them on the same level; they wouldn't see the difference. I mean, "It's got Black people in it so it's Black theatre."

I want to talk about producing plays in this system. This is one of the most corrupt systems in the world. You don't really know it until you get into it. A lot of you may not know it, but it costs more to produce a play nonprofit in New York than it costs to produce it for profit. For example, you can do a play with commercial investments in an Off-Broadway theatre for

$60,000—$70,000. But that same play in a nonprofit theatre may cost $100,000.

What you find out—and I'm saying this with caution, but I think it's true and I feel very strongly about it—is people who work in nonprofit institutions are basically lazy because they know they're going to get a check every week whether the play is a hit or not. In the commercial theatre, if it's not a hit, you don't get paid, you don't make anything. So they will *sell* you a ticket.

Control of commercial theatre in New York is by the theatre-going people on Broadway. If you deal with Off-Broadway, it's controlled by the *New York Times* and such. No matter how much you may think you can get through by not using the *New York Times,* they know if you open a play for $75,000, they are going to get $15,000 of that in ads. The theatre knows when you open a play on Broadway that they're going to get $12,000 a week. They don't care whether you have two people in the house or two thousand. That's the system we're operating under. You can do an all-Black play on Broadway with ten characters, and there will be twenty-five union white people who are making more than those ten actors, sometimes three times as much. And that's what's really frightening about this system.

Another thing I just wanted to say is that I used to read these magazines like *Theatre Arts* and all kinds of books that said the "Negro in American Theatre" this, or the "Negro in American Theatre" that, and somewhere in the mid-sixties that started changing to "Black Theatre Movement" and "Blacks in Theatre." It was mainly because . . . plays like *Anna Lucasta* were directed and produced by whites. Blacks in the Black theatre movement changed that to where Black people in plays projected unity. I point to theatre groups, producing organizations like the Frank Silvera Writers' Workshop— just staging plays—and places like Concept-East in Detroit and Free Southern Theatre, which deal exclusively with the audience in their development. Also there's the change in attitude from the mid-sixties with ourselves in terms of white people. During the mid-sixties, as I think somebody mentioned, Black actors in Detroit felt they were able to coerce the Detroit Repertory Theatre into doing a play where they would have leads. Now in the mid-seventies you can't coerce them anymore because they feel they don't need you anymore. Blacks are expendable in most white institutions. It wouldn't matter if you put on a play and turned away 200 people. If that play doesn't appeal to a white audience, then that play won't get on.

Someone mentioned "cross-over audience." I think one of the greatest fallacies in the last ten, twelve years is the "cross-over audience." If Black people packed a theatre for three or four months and paid to see it, white people would come and see that play whether you were in one of the worst ghettoes anywhere in New York; they will come and hate it, but they will come. I don't think that anyone should develop a play or a film because of its cross-over potential.

Trazana Beverley (left), Myrna White, Lynn Whitfield, Marylyn Coleman, and Aku Kadoga in *For Colored Girls Who Have Considered Suicide,* Los Angeles, 1978.

Anatomy of a
Successful Play

IN ORDER TO PRODUCE A PLAY,
it is necessary first to find the *right* play, and then to find the *money* to produce
it with. That money is what I want to talk about. The money is used to pay for
about thirty-five different items which cannot be listed in order of priority
because all are necessary. Now the play may be a one-set play or a five-set
play; it may have a cast of under ten or over ten. A producer can usually read a
play and tell within $5,000 what it will cost to produce under normal circum-
stances. Playwrights don't know what their plays cost to produce and usually
feel it's the producer's problem. Some are very bitter at their lack of success.
The few good writers who work *in* theatres or have their own acting companies usually write plays that are produceable. If a producer feels that a writer
or the problems that his play presents are not worth his time, *he will not
produce the play.*

It usually takes a Black producer about six months to raise $50,000. If the
play is moderately successful, it could take another six months to pay his
investors. That means the producer worked for a year and made no money
other than some expenses. That also means he must have some other means of
support. A $100,000 production can tie a producer up for as long as 20
months. A good producer wants to be paid for that kind of time, and he wants
to pay his investors back because if he can't pay the investors he can't go to
them again with ease and confidence.

Black investors, as a rule, cannot afford to lose their investment. Most
are hoping for a big hit. The corner grocery store, barbeque concept is out;
large chain supermarkets are in, underselling and putting small shops out of
business. Small Black operations cannot buck the big system. What happened
is this: some whites got together and financed twenty-five big markets across
the U.S. It costs less and, at the same time, it kills off the competition (the
supermarket versus the small neighborhood corner store). If a Black produces
a play and it is successful, whites will produce ten versions of it as quickly as
they can get to the bank. They have the investors at the ready.

(From left, clockwise) Woodie King, Jr. (author and producer), Ed Bullins (playwright), Michael
Schultz (director), and Lonne Elder III (playwright).

Most Black investors don't know the difference between the small nonprofit theatre that seats a few hundred and a Broadway theatre that houses *The Wiz*. In most cities with any kind of Black population, there is a Black theatre group struggling against all odds just to stay alive. Blacks who pay individual government taxes and corporate taxes are not aware that the tax returns are used to perpetuate white American arts and culture both directly and indirectly. If Black investors need the loss they can contribute it directly to the theatre groups and claim the investment loss themselves; if the investor wants a possible future profit or a future loss, he can invest in a *commercial* Black production such as *The Wiz* or *Bubbling Brown Sugar* or *What the Winesellers Buy*.

In the past ten years, the same Blacks who perform in the small community theatres often pop up on Broadway, Off-Broadway or in motion pictures. The same writers who write for the small theatres may write the screenplay for *Sounder* or *Let's Do It Again*. And for that reason, Black investors are at times confused by the two mediums as they relate to the almighty dollar. Small theatre groups, like the Negro Ensemble Company or the Inner City Cultural Center, are supported by foundation grants and patrons. In these nonprofit theatres, it's about building a lasting institution.

With a million dollars, each of the above-mentioned theatre groups could present ten productions and many workshops, while a commercial production like *The Wiz* might cost as much as a million dollars alone to produce. In both cases, a producer must find the money to make the play happen on stage. Since I operate in both arenas, I thought it useful to try and explain some of the problems. And since the problems in the nonprofit theatres are so familiar to the general public, I won't dwell on them for any length. I will say that if information is needed, the theatres must provide it to the general public upon written request, for any taxpayer can request information, both financially and otherwise, from any nonprofit theatre. Furthermore, any tax-exempt organization over two years old can apply for federal and state funding to present good art. Each local or national foundation has its own rules, and the grant depends on the local or national impact of the theatre requesting the money. All the foundations want visibility from their grants. They want names.

In a way it's no different from the Hollywood star system. The thin line between the nonprofit and the commercial at times can be frightening. The foundations are the root cause of the line being so thin. The producers of nonprofit theatres also must share a lot of the blame: they often select plays that are old standards, i.e., Tennessee Williams, Edward Albee, Arthur Miller, etc., in the white cases; in the Black cases, they select plays with those elements that leave the possibility of a commercial production open—small cast, provocative theme, hip characters, etc., all the while hoping for a *New York Times* rave and that it will be so successful that it won't be necessary to go back begging the foundations for money.

Financing for the commercial Black production comes from various sources. Usually white producers who've made money from other Black plays are the first contacts. Many of these producers don't have to use cash: they use letters of credit to banks that would not give a Black producer the time of day, even though the Black might use the bank exclusively for all his business. The bonds are all letters of credit. These bonds are for press agents, general managers, Actors Equity Association, and most of the craft unions. This can be as much as $50,000 of some budgets and as little as $10,000 on small Off-Broadway shows. These white producers rent their lights, props, some of the costumes on a thirty-day pay deal so that if the play opens in twenty days they can take the ten days of income and pay off some of the bills. If the play should close, bills will be paid at some future date. What would cost a Black producer $100,000 might cost a white producer $50,000 cash. The friendship between whites in the New York commercial theatre is unbelievably tight. The Shuberts are friendly with the Nederlanders, and the Alexander Cohen office is friendly with First American Theater Congress, etc. In short, the League of Broadway Producers is friendly with the League of New York Theater Owners. It is the same with all the craft unions. Until a Black producer moves the way these organizations feel he should move, he cannot produce in the New York theatre *without the actual cash*.

Financing a typical under-ten-character drama with one set goes something like this: The play must be optioned. The writer must be paid something. This amount can range from $1 to $500, depending on who the writer is and how badly the producer wants the play. An option does not mean the play will actually be produced; it means that a producer will take it off the market for six months trying to raise the other capital to actually present the play. Now, to do all this, a lawyer is needed. The lawyer's fee can range from $500 to $1,000. The lawyer will handle all agreements; each step of the way the lawyer will keep the producer aware of the prevailing regulations from the attorney general's office. A limited partnership will be formed. This partnership spells out investors' rights and privileges. It is about fifteen pages designed to protect the investor. Anything promised an investor outside of this agreement probably will be jive. Yet, the producer will have spent money getting the scripts copied, paid an option amount to the writer, and paid an attorney at least half his fee. This could be as much as $15,000 or as little as $500.

Let us say that the limited partnership is formed for a play that will cost $50,000 to open. That will mean each point or unit will be $1,000, for in a limited partnership there can be only fifty units. Take it a step further and use a limited partnership for a production that costs $100,000 and each unit will be $2,000. Since this amount can only get a producer to opening night, how then does the investor get his money back? And what does this $50,000 or $100,000 buy? Here is a typical budget:

author	$ 500	advertising	$7,500
director	1,000	art work	750
attorney	1,000	photo and signs	1,000
scenic designer	750	mailing	2,500
lighting designer	750	lighting	750
costume designer	750	costumes	2,000
accountant	500	props	700
general manager	1,000	set	5,000
actors		hanging	1,000
(10 × $150 × 4)	6,000	theatre bond	
stage manager		(6 wks at $1,500)	9,000
(1 × $250 × 4)	800	ATPAM (press agent	
assistant stage manager		and manager)	1,200
(1 × $175 × 4)	700	utility bond theatre	1,000
press agent	600	Actors' Equity	3,750
scripts	400	insurance	1,500
producer's expense	800	hospitalization and welfare	1,250
rehearsal space	800	legal advertising and disburse	1,500
general manager	1,000	tickets and programs	600
box office (one week)	250	payroll tax	1,700

This then, give or take a few hundred here or there, will be what it will cost to open a straight play Off-Broadway in New York. Usually the play opens on Tuesday, Wednesday, or Thursday, and if the reviews are bad it will close on Sunday. A wise producer tries to add a 20 percent contingency on a production budget of $50,000 or more. Thus, on the above budget, the limited partnership might be formed at $75,000, where each point would be $1,500. To do the same play on Broadway would cost about three times as much; to take the same play on tour would cost about twice as much. It's obvious the investor's return could be greater on Broadway or on tour. Seating capacity in both cases is four-to-one.

In order to keep a play open, once it has gotten decent reviews and people like it, poses another problem. Investors often wonder why they are not getting money even though the play is running every week. Because a play continues to operate doesn't mean it is making money. The weekly operating cost of a play is the most difficult because a producer must work constantly to keep an audience coming in the door. For an Off-Broadway theatre the weekly operating cost looks something like this:

actors (10 × $150)	$ 1,500	rent	1,500
stage manager	200	office charge	100
assistant stage manager	175	electric	100
press agent	300	wardrobe (clean)	75
producer's expense	250	food (cast)	75
general manager	300	insurance	150
box office	250	payroll taxes	400
understudy (2)	300	union benefits	250
crew (2)	300	rent tax	100
ushers (2)	150	set designer	50
secretary	150	light designer	50
porter	100	costume designer	50
advertising	3,000	audit	150
		director (2 percent)	200
		author (6 percent)	600

The play cannot remain open unless these bills are paid each week. In a few cases a producer might be able to convince the director and the author to waive their royalties until the box office receipts pick up. A producer must make his break-even cost or he must use his contingency. The only way the people who filled the positions can be paid each week is that enough people pay to see the play. No emotional rap about how good the play is, or how unfair the critics are, or how great the lead actor is, or how nice the producer is, matters after opening night.

How does the investor get his money back if the play is a hit? In a theatre Off-Broadway, with ticket prices at the $6 or $7, and $8 range, a straight play can break even at about $10,000 per week. If every seat is full every night, the theatre can gross about $18,000 per week, meaning a profit of $8,000 per week. In ten weeks, all the investors could be repaid their original investment. After that, the profits are divided 50 percent to all the investors and 50 percent to the producer. If the play continued at capacity, a producer could make almost $4,000 per week.

The same play on tour or *on* Broadway could break even at about $25,000 per week. However, at capacity, the Broadway theatres and the road theatres can gross as much as $100,000. Figuring that the play could be produced on Broadway for about $200,000, a possible weekly profit could be as much as $75,000. Repayment of original investment would be in about three weeks. After investors are repaid their original investment, a producer could make as much as $37,000 per week.

Now, all this may sound good on paper, and it may lead a few hustlers into producing, but here's a warning: the likelihood of this happening is very remote. In the past ten years, you can count on one hand the number of Black plays that jumped out and became gigantic hits. Most of the productions never pay back the original investment. Some excellent productions, like *The First Breeze of Summer,* lost the entire investment even though it played for ten weeks on Broadway. Ed Bullins' *The Taking of Miss Janie* had the distinction of being voted by the Drama Critics Circle as the Best New American Play of 1974-1975, yet it lost its entire investment. It has been said that both plays were in the wrong location for maximum Black visibility.

An investor also shares in what is called subsidiary rights of a play. Subsidiaries may be television sales, motion picture sales, stock and amateur productions and foreign productions. These rights can last up to ten years. Those who invested in Tennessee Williams' early plays are still collecting on the revival productions of the plays. If a play is sound, and if it has lasting qualities, it will be difficult for that play to fail.

If a producer has himself together legally, and if his play is positive, how does he go about getting it financed? Some go into partnership with other individuals who might have access to people who earn enough to give them the luxury of investing. A producer must locate people who earn $15,000 or more. They are the only ones who can safely afford to lose $500 or a $1,000. If they are single, with no dependents, it's likely they will have to return that amount to the government. Clubs and other organizations are also a good source for investments. Usually these organizations can easily invest $5,000 if they believe in the project. Always the contact with these organizations must be direct. It can never be by letter or telephone. If these groups are national, a large audience for the play follows their investment.

The small investors who put money into a play because they like it and because they themselves are involved in Black theatre are the most reliable in the Off-Broadway areas. Many of the plays that I've produced Off-Broadway were financed by other Black actors or artists. Most of them don't expect any return on their investment. They do it because they love the play and want to see it produced.

Even though I have never found the large businesses to be a source of investments, white producers tell me they've obtained investments through them. *The Me Nobody Knows* was financed partially through Seagram's whiskey. Another large musical, *1600 Pennsylvania Avenue,* was financed by Coca-Cola. The motion picture company, Twentieth Century- Fox, financed *The Wiz.* I produced a musical by J.E. Franklin and Mikki Grant called *The Prodigal Sister.* The cigarette company, R.J. Reynolds Tobacco, wanted to tour the production as a promotion for Salem cigarettes. On another musical, *Cotillion,* by John Killens, I was able to get the money from Motown to develop the novel into a book musical. However, in the end, they declined to put up the money for the show.

For my future productions, I will be setting up backers' auditions for major Black businesses. It is better to travel to other cities and have one of the leading players read the play than to try and make deals through the mail. In the past few years, Black businesses have shown some interest in the Black theatre. The commercial and noncommercial possibilities are being discussed at places like Black Enterprise, Motown, Atlanta Life Insurance, Uniworld Advertising Agency, and other companies in cities like Cleveland, Detroit, Philadelphia, Chicago, Atlanta, San Francisco, and Los Angeles. From most of these companies a small investment of $5,000 will be requested. If the play is successful, future investments can be more in line with the size of the production. Several theatre producers are already at work convincing the business group in New York known as the 100 Black Men that the theatre is a place for sound investments.

It is easier to make a businessman understand a good business deal. Explaining to someone who must make every decision on whether it is a sound business proposition rather than another emotional appeal tends to keep producers on their toes. Protecting an investor's money and at the same time presenting appealing and educational entertainment can be an exhilarating experience.

Legacy of A Raisin in the Sun:
Hansberry's Children

THREE YEARS AGO, NOT LONG
after *For Colored Girls Who Have Considered Suicide/ When The Rainbow is
Enuf* opened, when the Black musicals on Broadway were regarded as Black
theatre, I decided—out of anger—to make a documentary film on Black
theatre. The film had to begin at some point that was identifiable to the current
generation of theatre-goers and theatre artists. The reasonable and logical way
to do this, I surmised, would be to let each of the participants interviewed
decide his or her starting point.

What exactly do the following artists have in common: Lonnie Elder,
Lloyd Richards, Douglas Turner Ward, Ossie Davis, Ruby Dee, Robert
Hooks, Rosalind Cash, Ernestine McClenden, Ivan Dixon, Diana Sands,
Sharneille Perry, Ron Milner, and most of the young writers and performers
who are currently working in American theatre? The answer, without ques-
tion, is Lorraine Hansberry's *A Raisin in the Sun*. Hence the title of my film,
"The Black Theatre Movement: *A Raisin in the Sun* to the Present."

How to describe the effect *A Raisin in the Sun* had on most of us when it
opened in 1959! From my standpoint as a resident of Detroit who had only
recently become interested in theatre and had no guide whatsoever, *A Raisin
in the Sun* opened doors within my consciousness that I never knew existed.
There I was in Detroit's Cass Theatre, a young man who had never seen
anywhere a Black man (Walter Lee) express all the things I felt but never had
the courage to express—and in a theatre full of Black and white people, no
less! I remember being introduced by someone to Ron Milner in the lobby. We
both uttered something like, "This is it, man." And I remember waiting at the
stage door for *any* of the actors and finally cornering Robert Hooks (then
known as Bobby Dean Hooks). As we walked the ten or twelve blocks to his
hotel, he listened patiently to my enthusiastic outpourings—he didn't talk
much in those days. I remember showing him an article from *Theatre Arts
Magazine* and telling him how desperately I wanted to work in the profes-

sional theatre. My deep feelings came from the effect *A Raisin in the Sun* had had on me. Hooks laughed and said my feelings were not unique. When he had seen the play in Philadelphia, it had made him pack his bags and head for New York. Furthermore, in all of the cities the play had toured, young actors and actresses had been moved. The power of the play had made us all aware of our uniqueness as Blacks and had encouraged us to pursue our dreams. Indeed, the play had confirmed that our dreams were possible.

Sixteen years later, I interviewed over sixty people while filming my documentary on Black theatre. Over forty of those people said that, at one time or another, they had been influenced or aided, or both, by Lorraine Hansberry and her work. Consider, for example, the case of Lloyd Richards, director of the original *Raisin,* whose acceptance on the national theatre scene dates from that production. After *Raisin,* Richards directed many plays on Broadway and in university and regional theatres. None, however, had such wide exposure and impact as did Hansberry's work. He went on to serve as artistic director of the O'Neill Theatre Center in Waterford, Connecticut, and as president of the Theatre Development Fund. Currently, he heads Yale University's prestigious drama department. The very nature of *Raisin* and its overall message to all people made it possible for those who participated in its presentation to be embraced by both white and Black.

Whatever Sidney Poitier may feel, the role of Walter Lee Younger came at a time in his career when Black acceptance was extremely important—and elusive. His performance was a landmark and still must be considered one of the finest stage performances of an American actor. The same is to be said for the work of Claudia McNeil, Diana Sands, Ruby Dee and Glynn Turman. *A Raisin in the Sun* also made it possible for its author, Lorraine Hansberry, to speak out and be heard on issues of race where no other Black woman had been so treated (witness her famous meeting with Robert Kennedy, her articles and essays on Black aspirations, etc.). The effect all this had on the current crop of Black artists is tremendous, as evidenced in part by the female playwrights who have succeeded Hansberry—Adrienne Kennedy, J.E. Franklin, Aishah Rahman, Martie Evans-Charles, Elaine Jackson, Ntozake Shange and many others. To mention all of the artists whose careers were enhanced by their encounters with Hansberry and *A Raisin in the Sun* would read like a *Who's Who* in the Black theatre.

Early in my career, I performed in *A Raisin in the Sun* when a summer stock company came to Detroit's Northland Playhouse. I felt I had come full circle when, in 1978, I had the opportunity to direct the play with a talented cast headed by Minnie Gentry and Reuben Greene. (Evidence of the play's enduring effectiveness is the fact that it was just as well received in 1978 as it had been in that small Detroit theatre years earlier, when an overwhelmingly white audience gave it a standing ovation.) *Raisin* and I met again in January, 1979, in New York City when I produced the work at my New Federal Theatre—featuring, once again, the sterling Minnie Gentry. In the role of Walter Lee Younger was Glynn Turman. Significantly, Lorraine Hansberry had, twenty years earlier, personally escorted Turman (then her neighbor in Greenwich Village) to the audition that won him the role of twelve-year old Travis in the original Broadway production of *Raisin*. That Turman matured to star in the revival as an artist of award stature testifies, not only to his dedication and great ability, but also to the vision of Lorraine Hansberry.

Graham Brown and Frances Foster in *Behold! Cometh the Vanderkellans,* New York City. 1971.

A Conversation with Woodie King, Jr.

An interview by Earl Anthony
from *Players Magazine*, November 1980.

You are generally acclaimed *as the "premier" Black stage producer, with the possible exception of Ashton Springer. What are the stages in your career that have brought you to this point?*

Well, first of all, I don't consider myself the "premier" Black stage producer. I produce a lot of plays—they reach a lot of people. I started out, not out of a commercial kind of possibility, but out of a sheer need to get writers on stage who would not otherwise have had the opportunity to be seen. One of the things about producing is that there are plays that cry out to be done, that just beg to be done. Over the last decade you've seen some of the plays that would not have otherwise been done by the so-called "white market." Most of those plays ended up being very, very successful in the financial sense. I think that is what brought me to the attention of the theatre world, the Black world in particular and the "white" theatre world in general. If you look at plays like *Black Girl*, which ran for a year Off-Broadway; *Slaveship*, which brought Gilbert Moses, the renowned stage and film director into prominence; *What the Winesellers Buy;* and *For Colored Girls Who Have Considered Suicide/ When The Rainbow Is Enuf* you'll see they had a tremendous audience appeal—when in the beginning no one felt they would have that kind of appeal.

In the sixties you were recognized as one of the leaders of the Black Cultural Movement. How do you recall that experience?

The experience of working in the sixties was one of the most fruitful times of our history since the Black Renaissance of the twenties and thirties. We had more poets, writers, and artists working and being recognized.

Some people feel that the Black Cultural Movement was a rebirth of the Harlem Renaissance. What do you feel?

In a sense I feel that the Black Cultural Movement of the sixties had a lot to do with the same kind of feeling that was instilled in people regarding the renaissance of the twenties and thirties. If you read a book like Nathan Huggins, *The Harlem Renaissance,* you will see the systematic rip-off of Black culture by the white system. I don't want to condone or say that is something that definitely happened in the sixties but there was a lot of misguided energy. There was an enormous amount of positive energy guided in the right direction until any kind of negative aspect of the time must be looked on as coming from people who had not really "lived" through the sixties. If I deal with the criticism of the Black Cultural Movement of the sixties now, I would say it comes from people who came of age in the mid-seventies who are trying to make a place for themselves in the mainstream of the American system as cultural nationalists. What they really want is some sort of assimilation into the white world. Whether that be Hollywood, Broadway, or the music scene. You will not find the kind of in-depth work that was done in the Black community or the Black Cultural Movement during the sixties and in the Harlem Renaissance of the twenties and thirties.

Who are some of the people in the Black Cultural Movement considered to be personae that represent the 1960s?

In terms of my own feelings, Amiri Baraka (LeRoi Jones), as the main cultural force, Don L. Lee, and Malauna Ron Karenga from the West Coast. In terms of writers and playwrights there were Ronald Milner, Ed Bullins, Douglas Turner Ward, Lonnie Elder, and Lorraine Hansberry for her play *Raisin in the Sun* in 1959, and then again in the mid-sixties with *Sign In Sidney Brustein's Window;* Charles Gordone for his *No Place to Be Somebody.* Those were major works. There was a continuation of major novelists such as John A. Williams, John Oliver Killens, and always the Pan-African thought and feelings that were instilled in all of us by the work of John Henri Clark. The two main works of cultural revolution were by Martin Luther King and Malcolm X, whose autobiography has become the Bible of cultural and economic revolution. This came about through his growing up and his assassination in the mid-sixties.

You have also been involved in the publishing industry. Can you tell us about that?

Again my involvement was in the late sixties and early seventies. I published some of the most important collections of Black literature. *A Black Quartet* was one of the first collections of Black plays by revolutionary Black writers Ed Bullins, Ben Caldwell, Amiri Baraka (LeRoi Jones), and Ron Milner. We also did *The Anthology of Black Drama* for Signet Books, which included some of the leading writers such as Joseph Walker, Douglas Turner Ward, Ed Bullins, Elaine Jackson, Martie Evans-Charles, and we could go on and on. We did a collection of short stories in the early seventies by some of the major Black short story writers, called *Black Short Story Anthology*. In addition, I did *Forerunners* for the Howard University Press which listed some fifteen major poets that we learned from such as Sterling Brown, Robert Hayden, Charles Wright, Margaret Danner, and Margaret Burroughs, just to name a few. It was the kind of work that I think spoke out for the period of time in which they were created. The theories, practices, and aesthetics of the Pan-African Movement or "Black Poets and Prophets" as it was called was put together by Earl Anthony and me and for the first time compiled under one cover the works of Stokely Carmichael, Ron Karenga, Sekou, Toure, Franz Fanon, and Anthony. This was a major commitment in the mid-seventies when it was difficult to get that kind of work past the industry. Those are the five books that I edited and put together in my publishing period.

You showcased and produced Ntozake Shange's Broadway and national blockbuster, For Colored Girls Who Have Considered Suicide/ When The Rainbow Is Enuf. *How did that come about?*

I had read pieces of Ntozake Shange's work in the *Black Scholar* and a lot of other poetry publications for about three or four years, and I really liked what I read. We had originally produced a play by her sister Efa, and we presented it here at the playhouse and she came in and talked to us about it and introduced Ntozake to us. *Colored Girls* was brilliantly put together by stage director, stage manager O. Z. Scott.

So, when he brought *Colored Girls* to us I jumped at it because it had been a project I had been trying desperately to put together for some time, something that made a statement directly to women in general and about poetry. We put the play on here at the New Federal Theater—and it was a blockbuster. We had lines around the block. We hooked up with Joseph Papp in a co-production deal and we moved the play to Broadway. It ran for two years and went on tour. I have produced it in Australia and three or four months ago in London to a tremendous success—in addition to the national company which toured the United States.

What are your other memorable stage productions?

I would have to say *What the Winesellers Buy* is certainly one of the productions I cherish. The play *Colored Girls,* Ed Bullins' *The Taking of Miss Janie,* which won for us the Drama Critics Circle Award, and three Obie Awards. I would have to include one of my first productions, Earl Anthony's *Charlie Can't Win No Wars on the Ground,* and *The Misjudgment,* dealing with young revolutionaries. Everyone remembers Anthony's plays because of the crisp and brilliant writing. Kirk Kirksey's Obie Award-winning performance as a Muslim was a memorable moment in *Charlie.* I feel good about a play we did called *Show Down Time* by Don Evans, and Martie Evans-Charles' *Jemima* starring Dick Williams, who was also the star of *What the Winesellers Buy.* Going back a few years I would say Sonny Jim James' *Don't Let It Go to Your Head,* and Charles Fullers' *In My Many Names and Days* was sort of a monumental task, to do five plays over one weekend—and it ran for one month. It was one of the few plays we did that was nominated for a Pulitzer Prize.

You are also an actor. Would you tell us about some of your stage and film roles?

In the early sixties a lot of my work was Off-Broadway. I worked in the award-winning play by Douglas Turner Ward, *A Day of Absence.* I was in Charlie Fullers' *The Perfect Party* and then I went to Broadway to appear in the *Great White Hope* and several other plays in regional theatre. In the late sixties and early seventies I went into the television commercial acting world earning at different times upwards of $150,000 a year. I was one of the most visible commercial actors in the business. I only eased up when the cigarette commercials went off the air. I also appeared in several films including: *Move* with Ron O'Neil and Elliott Gould which was a terrible flop. I appeared in *Serpico* with Al Pacino and broke my leg in a chase scene; that told me to ease up while doing a film and I decided to make a more impressive track record in producing.

What are your latest stage projects?

My latest stage project is *Reggae.* It depicts the history and development of the Reggae music scene. Calvin Lockhart, Phillip Thomas, Sheryl Lee Ralph, and Olatunji are its very talented stars. Unfortunately, it closed because of the transit subway strike; it will reopen again soon. I am also producing Stevie Wonder's *Wonderland,* directed by Michael Shultz in December or January. I have been working on this project for some time and I'm especially pleased that I have been selected by Stevie Wonder to be the producer of his first Broadway play. The heart of the play will be centered around his last five albums, in addition to a great deal of bridging work being done by Stevie himself.

You are a "renaissance man" and have produced music albums as well as musical productions, could you tell us about that?

I don't know about being a "renaissance man"—that makes me sound like someone very old—I just started in the business very young and I hope I am still young in ideas and thoughts. I produced albums for Motown, under the Black Forum label. The Last Poets and Amiri Baraka's award-winning album, *Nation Time*, were very successful.

You produced, directed, and wrote a documentary for PBS also.

Actually, I produced and directed three films in four years. The first film was *The Long Night*, starring Dick Williams, Sonny Jim Gaines, Woody Jeffery King, Peggy Kirk Patrick, Roger Furman, and Shaunielle Perry. It was the only film selected for the New Directors Film Series at Lincoln Center. Two years ago I produced and directed a documentary film, *Black Theatre Movement*, that was subsequently shown over fifteen PBS stations which had interviews from across the U.S. including New York, California, South America and the Caribbean, winning the Black Film Maker Hall of Fame, First Award for documentary section in 1979. I have just completed another documentary called *The Torture of Mothers*, starring Ruby Dee, Clarice Taylor, Novella Nelson, Juanita Clark, and Starletta DuParr. The film is based on Truman Nelson's book about the Harlem Six, six boys who were accused of killing a white woman in Harlem during the early part of 1964. I tried to document the feeling and temper that actually took place in the Harlem community of the sixties.

You are one of the founding fathers of the Black theatre movement. Would you describe the motivation behind its conception?

The Black theatre movement came out of a need for Black artists to express whatever they felt in theatrical terms without doing the explaining to white people; especially when we were hoping to get a Black audience. In the last ten years I hope that most of the productions seen on Broadway—in terms of Black art—were some sort of guide to those people who felt the Black theatre movement would not last; that it was only a passing fad and the people who were being trained would not in a sense be able to do anything other than that. If you look at the work of most of the people in Hollywood, most of the actors in the last *Roots* came out of this same movement. Of course major directors such as Gil Moses, and Michael Shultz came out of it as well. Writers such as Lonne Elder, Richard Wesley and Ed Bullins. Lonne Elder came out of the Negro Ensemble Company. Again, what most of us in the theatre movement try to do is deal with our stories honestly, hoping that a Black audience will become a part of that honesty, and leave the theatre feeling better than when they came in. That is the idea. I'm not talking about a lot of plays that were written to chastise, harass, and make white people feel uncomfortable; I'm talking about major works that were about enlightenment, about consciousness-raising, about something in particular. If that means that I was there when all of it began—well, yes I was there but it was because there was nowhere else to be.

What is the status of the Black theatre movement now?

Across the United States, in every major city you will find major Black theatres. In Cleveland (The Karamu House), San Francisco, Concept-East in Detroit, the Free Southern Theatre in New Orleans, the Just US Theatre in Atlanta, Inner City in Los Angeles—it is a national movement, a major force.

What are your future plans?

My plans for the future are to do more and more theatre. I'm going to do one film a year. My next film is about the rhythm and blues music of the fifties, where I would go out and talk to many of the do-wop groups that are still around. We wanted to find out why the white record companies who produced them are wealthy and they are poor. Most of the groups of this era wrote, arranged, and sang their own material. Why have they failed to move through the years as a lot of the white groups have done? Why have they not been able to bridge the gap of rhythm and blues to what is now called soul? I am very interested in groups like the Spaniels, Little Anthony and the Imperials, the Cadillacs, the Midnighters and especially performers such as Hank Ballard. I will be talking to all of them to get a first-hand view of what really happened, what life is like for them now—and their future plans.

Then I will also be doing a comedy film called *The Beast of Harlem* where Harlem junkies are turned into beasts after taking some bad dope. As I mentioned earlier, my major project now is *Wonderland,* the Stevie Wonder project scheduled to begin the end of 1980. I will continue to work and produce the National Black Touring Circuit where I will be doing two plays in '82, three in '83, and four plays in '84. The New Federal Theatre at Henry Street is now ten years old and we will have a ten-year anniversary celebration starting in November. It will last two months and we hope to have many of the people who came out of our theatre come back a couple of hours and feel good about the past and better about the future we all share.